TOP MARK!

TOP MARK!

An Autobiography

MARK HATELEY
with
KEN GALLACHER

MAINSTREAM
PUBLISHING

EDINBURGH AND LONDON

First published in Great Britain in 1993 by
MAINSTREAM PUBLISHING COMPANY
(EDINBURGH) LTD
7 Albany Street
Edinburgh EH1 3UG

ISBN 1 85158 593 1

A catalogue record for this book is available from the
British Library

Typeset in Palatino by Litho Link Ltd, Welshpool, Powys
Printed in Great Britain by Butler & Tanner Ltd, Frome,
Somerset

Other Mainstream books by Ken Gallacher:

Field of Dreams with Richard Gough
Strachan Style with Gordon Strachan
Tall, Dark and Hansen with Alan Hansen
A Manager's Diary with Graeme Souness
Jousting with Giants with Jim McLean
Paradise Lost with David Hay

To a childhood sweetheart and my family,
who have made all this possible.

Contents

CHAPTER ONE

The Roar of the Crowd

It took me a long time to get to Ibrox and, after a few false starts, when I did join Rangers, I wondered for a short spell if it had been the right move. Not because I had doubts about the club's status or about the club's ambitions, but simply because I was caught up in the row over who should be playing with me as the first-choice strike force – something I'll deal with in the next chapter. Once that little local difficulty had disappeared, I had no doubts in my mind that, once again, I had taken the career move which was right for me at that stage of my career.

Twice before, Graeme Souness had tried to buy me – and each time he had failed. Even earlier, John Greig had made an approach for me when I was still a very young player with Coventry. I didn't know about that at the time. John told me when I eventually signed with Rangers. He had been friendly with the Coventry manager, Gordon Milne, and his right-hand man, Ron Wylie, and he had been at Highfield Road to look at the training and the whole set-up there. The word among the players at the time was that he was after another of the club's strikers, Gary Thompson. Instead, John tried to buy me, but his offer was rejected by the club. So I moved on to Portsmouth, to AC Milan and to Monaco before finally getting to Rangers.

In the meantime, Graeme had tried to get me when I was leaving Milan. Other Italian teams were after me but the new Milan president, Silvio Berlusconi, who wanted me out, also wanted to make sure that I did not return to the San Siro stadium to haunt him with some other club in Serie A. He wanted me out of the country, and so Roma and Verona, two Italian sides who were trying to sign me, were ruled out. Graeme put in a bid but so too did Monaco, and at that stage I decided that the best move for me was to go to Prince Rainier's club. As well as Rangers, the German side Bayern Munich were interested, as were Arsenal and Manchester United.

Then, after my first season in the French First Division, Graeme was back with another offer. We had just won the League and the European Cup was looming, but Graeme is a man who can be very persuasive when he wants to be, and he talked Monaco into allowing him to have signing discussions with me. He came over with the then chairman, David Holmes, and Walter Smith was there too, and we sat down together and hammered out personal terms. Everything was looked after – even down to the colour of the kitchen we would have in the house which Rangers were going to help us find.

Then, suddenly, there was silence. It all went ominously quiet. Graeme had phoned with a formal bid – matching the kind of money that Monaco had indicated they were looking for – and I thought it would just be a formality. But someone at Monaco had doubts about the wisdom of selling me and there was a change of heart. Graeme went back to them with what I presumed was an increased offer, but it made no difference. The deal went dead on us. For a month or so I did not hear a single whisper about the transfer, not even a hint

14

of what might be going on behind the scenes. Then suddenly, out of nowhere, Monaco sent me a letter which offered an extension to my contract and proposal to double my wages at the same time. So there I was, clutching my first ever winner's medal after the French League title the previous season, with the chance to play in the European Cup in the coming season and with a fabulous new wages deal available. I sat down with my wife, Beverly, and talked it all through. We had three more years of living in paradise in front of us and now we had all this extra money too. There was also the beguiling thought that there was no income tax to be paid in Monaco and we had idyllic surroundings.

What's more, the club *wanted* me to stay. They *wanted* me to remain as a key player for them over the next few seasons – and that's always important when you are deciding your future. Then, of course, I was still under my original contract and if they had decided that I was staying as their player then there was simply nothing I could do about it.

Only one flaw remained in the whole thing – and that was that by this time I was no longer enjoying my football there. That was one of the major reasons why I wanted to make the move to Glasgow and to Rangers. I happen to be the type of player who thrives on a relationship with the fans. I enjoy all of that – giving them something to cheer about and then getting something back from them with their support. I love to hear the roar of the crowd. I love to hear the songs and the chants and I love to get myself involved. There is nowhere quite like Ibrox for that on a big match day. And despite the problems I had at the start, these fans have been magnificent to me. Right away I can remember vital games, really crucial games, when they have inspired the team: winning the title against Aberdeen on the last day of my first season with the club was one; coming back from the dead against Marseille in the European Champions' League and doing the same in the earlier Ibrox clash with Leeds United when we had lost that early goal; and this season when we were down to ten men against Celtic in the semi-final of the League Cup and yet were still able to win the game . . . There have been more occasions when the fans have lifted us, but these are a few I remember vividly – and there was never that kind of feeling among the mega-rich residents of Monaco.

I have been fortunate – or you could say I have been shrewd – in the moves I have made during my career. Each one seems to have arrived at a juncture in my life when that particular transfer and the club I chose was right for me. Even as a young player when I went to Portsmouth from Coventry, there were some people around who were convinced that I had done the wrong thing. I was dropping down a division and that wasn't reckoned to be the brightest thing to do. Other clubs wanted me. Chelsea and Queen's Park Rangers would have bought me and so, surprisingly in the light of his later assessments of my ability, did Graham Taylor at Watford. I picked Portsmouth, shocked a few people, and went there to learn my trade as a striker under the guidance of the manager, Bobby Campbell. It was the fact that Bobby was there that made it such a good move for me – and, eventually, such an important move too, because he made me the player I am today and have been down through the years since. It was thanks to Bobby that I was able to go abroad and be a success there, thanks to him that I won my England caps and thanks to him, too, that I was able to end up with Rangers.

Bobby bought me so Bobby believed in me, but he was always on at me to get more aggression into my play. He used to tell me that I had to be 'more horrible' on the park. He demanded that I should be more commanding when I was leading the line. He wanted to see me use my height and my strength because – while some centre-halves may not believe this – I did not use these physical attributes nearly enough when I was a kid. It wasn't in my make-up back then – Bobby Campbell put it there. He saw the advantages I had and he told me that I was not using them enough. For him, they were being under-played. I had a year with Bobby when he made me so much more aware of my own strength and also of the pace I possessed. He had me work on that and develop it and use it to much better advantage than I'd ever done before.

I had a great time there and teamed up with Alan Biley and bagged a lot of goals and pushed my way into the England Under-21 side and the full side. But, most important of all, I attracted the interest of the Italian giants, AC Milan. I had left Coventry virtually an unknown – certainly a complete nobody outside my own country, and by working at my game at Portsmouth and developing those parts of my play which Bobby made me realise had been neglected, my career took off. Even now it's hard to believe how it all happened. But the strengths I developed, which are often bad-mouthed in this country, carried me into the biggest League in the world.

There is sometimes a greater appreciation of the British-style game abroad than there is here at home. Parts of our game are envied by the Italians and the French and others too – I learned that at first hand in the years I spent on the Continent. In Italy I used a great deal of what Bobby Campbell had preached to me and I added some refine-ments during my time there. The basic thing I'm trying to say here is that the Italians and the French were the same – they liked the idea of having a target-man. A big powerful British striker was what they wanted. I fitted the bill and, luckily, the Milan fans took to me immediately. In my first game against Udinese we could only draw 2–2 but I made one of our goals for Virdis and scored one myself with a back-post header. Two weeks later, in my second home match at the San Siro, we beat Cremonese 2–1 and this time I helped myself to both goals. The first was a header, the kind of goal the Italians were expecting from me. The second was a left-foot shot just to prove to them that I could play on the deck as well . . .

I had a marvellous time in Milan with the fans. They took to me and I enjoyed the adulation you get out there. The one problem they had was with my second name. They could not pronounce Hateley and so it came out of eighty thousand throats sounding like 'Attila', and that is where I got my nickname over there. The start could not have been better, nor could the reception. From Coventry and Portsmouth to the drama and constant excitement of the San Siro was to be catapulted into a different football world. And I loved every moment of it.

That may have been why I took so badly to the staid and near silent crowds in Monaco. But again, at the time, the move seemed the right one, and financially that was also the case. Just as it had felt right for me to undertake the Italian adventure, so it was right now, when Milan wanted me out of the country, to move across the border to Monaco. There was a challenge there, too. Monaco wanted to find success again after being without a major trophy win for around a decade. My problem – and it became one which nagged at me in game after game – was the lack of atmosphere at the matches. It did not matter how well we were playing, or how close we were to winning the title or the French Cup, the people just didn't turn up. The team and the game of football were passions for Prince Rainier and for his son Prince Albert, who used to train with us sometimes. But that passion didn't move far outside the walls of the Royal

Palace. Mind you, it has to be remembered that there are only 28,000 people in Monaco and because there are some seriously wealthy tax exiles among them you could find maybe just fifteen or twenty thousand in the principality on a day when we were playing. And it was a nightmare for anyone else to drive to as access was very difficult – and so we found ourselves playing to just a few thousand fans at the games. After the huge crowds in Italy and the ferocity of the atmosphere at a Milan derby with Inter, it was not too easy to adjust. I had to remind myself constantly that the offer I had accepted was one which guaranteed my future. I had to look at the lifestyle we enjoyed, living in a place which most people in Britain can only dream about visiting and where only very few can consider living on a permanent basis. For the family and for the future, nothing could have been better. For the football, though, there was a lot to be desired. I actually began to look forward to the away games because, as potential title-winners and one of the most attractive sides in the French First Division, we drew huge crowds – particularly if we were playing away to Nice or Marseille in what were considered to be local derby games.

It was a special place for the family and we were treated superbly. We had sunshine, luxury and great food – and Beverly was even on chatting terms with Princess Caroline when she used to take the kids out for a walk and meet her in the street or in the park. It was so laid-back and so wonderful for family life – but I grew more and more disenchanted. I was lucky that Glenn Hoddle was there at the same time because we could relate to each other just as I had been able to do with Ray Wilkins in Italy. He had been on the verge of signing for Paris St Germain, but there was a hitch in that deal which I heard about and tipped off Monaco. They moved in and within a couple of days Glenn had joined me. It is always best, I think, to have someone with you from your own country when you're playing abroad, and that helped me through any gloomy days I had in Monaco. Having Glenn around was one boost; winning the title was another. That was the first winner's medal I had picked up and I wasn't to see another until I joined Rangers.

It was early in my second season, just months after Monaco had turned down the bid from Graeme Souness and Rangers, that a blow struck which changed the whole direction my career was taking. Until then, I had been in control of my footballing life. I had decided to go to Portsmouth *against* some advice. I had decided to gamble on making the leap from the English Second Division to Serie A and sign for AC Milan. I had also chosen to go to Monaco to get the financial security I wanted for my family and to look for some personal success in the game at the same time.

All these moves had worked out, even though the poor crowds at Monaco continued to eat away at my appetite for the game. Still, I had a Championship medal and no worries for the future, and I knew I could hold out for at least another year of my contract before looking for a fresh challenge and a chance to play in front of passionate fans once more.

While I was trying to concentrate on doing well in the European Cup and also attempting to look beyond that to another season and perhaps the chance of a move, I was struck by the first of two dreadful injury blows. I wasn't to know it then, but this was a prelude to eighteen months of despair.

The one consolation which I can take from these dark days now is that, at the end of it all, I came to Rangers. Without the injuries I might not have made it to Ibrox and I might never have been able to find out for myself how wonderful the fans can be. I've played in the Milan derby games between AC and Inter and nowadays there are far more people able to attend these games than can go to the Old Firm clashes in Glasgow. But I know which games I would prefer to take part in. No matter that you have near enough double the number of people at the Milan matches, the tension in Glasgow is greater. The whole atmosphere is so different and so much more electric. At Ibrox or Celtic Park the passions go with the ebb and flow of the game and you can sense that. When you remember the pace of matches in Scotland, you realise what an emotional roller-coaster of a game you take part in. In Italy it is not like that and there is less singing and chanting and the mood doesn't swing as dramatically between one side and the other.

I've always liked to look on myself as a working man's footballer, someone who will give everything he has got to please the fans, the people who pay my wages. And I have never felt it more than I do in Glasgow with Rangers. I want to do well for them because I know how much a victory means to them – especially in an Old Firm game. Maybe it's because I find myself caught up in the passion of the occasion. Maybe it's because an age-old city rivalry like the one which exists between Rangers and Celtic is the life-blood of this game.

I don't know where else you could match that passion – and I've been around. I've played in the Maracana and in all the grounds in France and Italy and I've never known such fervour. It makes me want to give something back and I'm glad there have been times when I have done that because the Rangers fans – despite the little local difficulties in the beginning – helped rebuild my whole career. I'll always owe them something for that.

The day that Graeme and chairman David Murray came to see me in Monaco turned out to be one of the best days of my life.

CHAPTER TWO

Ally, Mo and Me

It seems strange now after the so profitable partnership that Ally McCoist and myself have struck up over the past fews years that it took us so long to get together . . .

At the time, when I arrived at the club from Monaco in the summer of 1990, it was even stranger. Here I was coming to Ibrox as another of the £1 million signings made by Graeme Souness, and not being flavour of the month with the fans. In fact, I found myself in the middle of a hornets' nest which was certainly not of my own making. It was not the easiest of times for me and I needed all the help and support I could get. A great deal of that support came from Graeme Souness, who had signed me and thrust me into the middle of a squabble about who should be playing in the first team as the strike force.

As far as I was concerned, I knew that my position was safe in that eternal soccer triangle because I knew why Graeme had signed me. In the summer, when he had come to Monaco for talks while the World Cup was taking place in Italy, he had explained that he wanted a player who would lead the line. I knew what he meant okay. After all, he had signed other front players in a bid to get the kind of striker he wanted up front. He had bought Colin West – I think that was his first signing in fact – and he also bought Mark Falco at another stage. Plus, when he did get me, it was at the third attempt. He had an obsession about a big, powerful hit-man – or target-man, as my kind of player tends to be called. So whatever happened, I was going to be playing first-team football and the quarrel was over which of the two other strikers at the club was going to be playing off me.

The unfortunate thing for me was that the fans didn't quite see it in these terms. And when Alastair was the player Graeme decided to axe, the trouble really erupted and I was caught in the middle of it all. Now that I know more about the situation in Glasgow and the controversy which surrounded the signing of Maurice Johnston, I'm absolutely convinced that if Mo had been dropped then there would have been little or no fuss. But Graeme was never a man to take the easy way out. He thought that Mo and myself would make the best partnership and that was the end of it as far as he was concerned. He was not about to change his mind because several thousand fans in the enclosure had decided that he was wrong.

Indeed, if those supporters who booed and jeered Mo and I in those months we played together had given things a thought, they would have realised that the more they yelled abuse, the more determined Graeme would become. If ever there was a way calculated to make Graeme Souness stick to a decision, it would be to publicly question him. In this case, though, Graeme thought he was right. None of this helped me with the fans. They looked at the team sheet, saw my name there, and decided that I was taking Coisty's place. And that was not going to be accepted. So while Alastair sat on the bench for the first few months, I was getting abuse from the enclosure supporters. To be honest, it didn't bother me too much. I had just spent close to eighteen months out of the game altogether because of injuries. To be back playing at the top level with a major club after all the worries I had been through was good enough for me. Things got so bad, though, that Graeme stood up at the club's annual meeting of shareholders, which was held soon after the season began, to ask for a fair deal for me.

As far as I was concerned, the worst part of it was that I had come to Rangers hoping to strike up a relationship with the supporters. I had had that at AC Milan during the time I spent in Italy and, as I said in the last chapter, I had missed out on it when I was at Monaco. It was not that the fans didn't give me tremendous support in my first season there when we won the title – it was just that there were so few of them. Even taking the title we were looking at six or seven thousand people scattered around the magnificent stadium. They like their football okay, but there are simply not enough people in the principality to give the team the support it should get – and would get if the same side was playing in any of the other major soccer venues in the French First Division. So when it didn't happen for me right away with the Rangers fans, it hurt. I had to dig deep inside myself to get the strength you need to play through that kind of situation. I didn't like it. No player does. But I do realise now that most of that early unpleasantness came through a combination of circumstances and from a minority of the fans. In the years since they have all been marvellous to me.

Despite what outsiders often think, there was no aggro in the dressing-room. There rarely is in these circumstances because good professionals know that they have to buckle down to whatever job they are given and get on with things. That can mean going into the team and getting stick from the fans, or being left sitting on the bench for almost a whole year as Alastair was. But players recognise that this can happen to anyone in the game. No one is guaranteed a career in any first team without interruption. Not even the greatest player of all can go on for ever, and that thought is always with you.

Eventually it became easier for me to deal with the situation than it was for the other two. They knew all along that it was a case of three into two won't go – and they knew, too, that I was always going to be first choice. When the fans finally realised that as well I began to get some peace. It took some time to win them over, but in the end it was worth while. The duel between Alastair and Mo went on for a little bit longer. I have to say that I admired Coisty's professionalism all the way through. It must have been a nightmare for him – and yet in the dressing-room there were few signs of the agonies he must have been suffering in private. It said a lot for his strength of character that he was able to keep going the way he did.

Essentially, of course, Alastair is a bubbly character and because of that he could put on a brave face even when things must have looked bleak. And deep down, he must have known in his heart of hearts that things were not going to change easily. He must have realised that Graeme was not going to change his mind suddenly and put him into the team in front of Maurice. That was not a possibility and Alastair, who is bright and intelligent, knew it better than most. Yet, despite the disappointment he must have felt week after week, he was still there and still ready to play when he was given the chance. His problem, really, was that the chances were few and far between.

Other players would have jacked it in, I'm quite sure of that. Some top players would not have taken kindly to being left out on a regular basis. They would have asked for a transfer or made it known how unhappy they were. It's never an easy thing for any player to train all week and then at the end of the hard graft, after preparing yourself to play in the team, take a back seat. And while players don't see it as people outside the game do, it still hurts that there are fans who consider it to be a public humiliation when a top-class player is simply not given the chance to play first-team football.

As well as his club career, Ally had his Scotland career to consider, too. Yet he never broke cover, never caused any public row, never asked for a transfer and never, ever put himself in the position of letting the club down. Nor did he let any of the players down. I think that he showed, in those long, long months, what he was made of and what his feelings were for Rangers. There is no doubt that he could have embarrassed the club and Graeme Souness because of the very obvious public support he had. He didn't do it. And, in the dressing-room, he was the one who still kept the jokes going. In fact, he was the player who came up with the nickname 'The Judge' for himself because he was spending so much time sitting on the bench.

Football is a job like any other, and in different walks of life people can often face the same problems: a new man comes into a business and put someone else's job at risk – that must happen every day of the week somewhere in the country. The difference is that the fellow in an ordinary job does not have to face the publicity which surrounds a top footballer who is suddenly, and sometimes brutally, axed. In a business you have to fight to keep your job – just as in football you have to battle to keep your place at the top. The difficulty is that a footballer does his fighting in the headlines, especially in Glasgow where football means so much. That's why it was so hard for Alastair and why I have nothing but admiration for him in the way he handled things. It was never up to me to say anything about the controversy, or to try to suggest which front-line partner I should have. I was new to the club and I had a big enough job on my hands to resurrect my own career and win over the fans. All I knew for sure was that I was to partner one or the other, and going there initially I had no real preference. Both players were Scottish internationals, both had goal-scoring reputations and both were the type of player who could live off a big, strong hit-man like myself. Graeme had wanted that type of partnership and had told me so. But he had not confided to me which of the men he had was going to be my front-line foil.

Unfortunately for myself and Alastair, the fans' favourite was the one who was left out at first. Actually, Maurice and I struck up a profitable partnership in that first season. This was the pairing Graeme Souness preferred and we got on with the job of helping the team get results. It took a long time, but finally things sorted themselves out and Alastair and myself came together. When we did, we hit it off as if we had been playing together for years. That was how it seemed and maybe it was because, by the time his chance came, Alastair had been watching me from the bench in so many games he knew how I liked to play. We got goals straight away and we are still scoring them regularly as I write now. Indeed, we worked so well together that we were able to get more goals than had been the case when I was with Maurice. I was getting more personally, and Coisty was getting more than Maurice had done – to be honest, he was getting more than *anyone* else would have done. His two Golden Boots have underlined that. These signify success and recognition at the highest level and he has really worked for them. These awards are so well deserved because of Alastair's determination in the dark days and for the way he handled himself then. It must have been the toughest time of his football career and no one admires him more than I do for the way he came through it all.

Actually, it was never going to be all that easy for Coisty to get back into the side in that first season because I did have a good partnership with Maurice, too. When I arrived I would say that, of the two players, Maurice had the better work-rate. He was at his best then, just a season back from playing in France, and he would just run and run and run. He was giving 110 per cent then, and with me just returning after my injuries and the subsequent problems, he was like a breath of fresh air. He was at a peak and he was very sharp and his weight was way down and he just wanted to play. Later, in the second season we were together, I saw a change in Maurice. He was not working as hard then and when Coisty got his chance he took it. By then there was not the slightest doubt in my mind that he *would* take it. He was hungrier than Maurice was by that stage. I didn't have any doubts, either, that Maurice would not suffer in silence the way Alastair had done if he was left on the bench for long periods. I was right.

Maurice carried his own pressures at the club and I think they were long term. I doubt if he would ever have been free of them. A section of the supporters just would never have accepted him fully no matter how well he might do or how many goals he might score. As well as that, he was a different kind of person from Coisty. There was never any way he could ever have accepted being left out of the team. That was just his way. If Graeme had left him out way back at the beginning, he would have been off earlier. It was just in his nature that he would not sit out games and patiently hope for a break to arrive which would allow him to regain his place. He was always going to be unhappy and he would let people know that. He spoke to the manager (by now, Walter Smith had replaced Souness) and the next thing we knew he was off to Everton.

The rest is history – Alastair and I have formed the most profitable partnership I have ever known, and I would like to think that he agrees with that. I don't think it's just in the number of goals we score, although that is always the main yardstick. It's also in the way we have learned to work together for the good of the team. I have improved my game by watching him and he has no doubt benefited from looking at some of the things I do. So much so that I rate him as the best player I have ever been asked to partner – and I have been with some of the best strikers in the game, believe me. I like to think I know what I am talking about when it comes to front players.

When I first signed for Rangers my impression was that Alastair was just an out-and-out goal-scorer. He was a penalty-box predator. All his work was done inside the eighteen-yard line and outside of that he didn't seem to have the same appetite for the game. That has changed dramatically over the last year or two. His general play, his play outside the penalty-box, has improved enormously. I think he has learned how to link up better with other players, whereas before he was simply content to get on the end of things around goal. For my part, I have learned to be a little bit more selfish in the box. He has taught me that. I will now have a go for goal whenever I think I have a scoring chance, while beforehand I might have tried to play it off to him. It has meant that, as a twosome, we have been able to hoist our scoring rate. Alastair gets the bulk of the goals because he is such a deadly finisher, but I now get my share to the extent that we scored just short of eighty goals between us last season. In doing all of this, we have been able to build up an almost telepathic understanding. That comes from experience and also from instinct. The more you play together, the more you know what to expect from the player who is at your elbow.

We have probably both become better, more complete players in the process of putting together our partnership.

That is the way it should be. Good professionals should always be able to learn from others – and should always be willing to do so. You are never too old or too good to be able to pick up something new in this game. I learned a lot in Italy when I was a young player, and here at Ibrox I am still learning about the job I do. I reckon that's why the pairing has been so good for the club and for both of us as players – we listen to each other and we watch each other and we react to each other. I just wish we had got together a little bit earlier.

I also tend to believe that Alastair is a much better player when he has a target-man up there with him. I have seen him criticised over his performances for his country but he has never had the proper foil when he has been playing international football. I don't think he always realised that himself; but, for me, he was born for that kind of pairing. The time we have played together has possibly convinced him that he does react better to having someone like myself with him. The way things have gone, I am not firmly of the opinion that Alastair would be able to hold his own with any of the top strikers I have come across in my time in the game.

When I first went to Italy, for example, I teamed up with Pietro Paolo Virdis, who was an exceptional player. He had been with Juventus previously and had always been a kind of fringe international player. He pushed his way into the Italian squad and played the odd game for them, but somehow, I could not really understand why, he was never able to command a regular place. He could never quite make that jump from club to international football as convincingly as he should have. He was a tremendous finisher and in that League you had to be able to take the slightest chance because you never got all that many. There was never too much room for error because you only had a very limited amount of goal chances, and Virdis was able to put away something like fifteen or sixteen goals in that first season I was there.

Then I had Paolo Rossi join me when he was approaching the end of his career. He was a big, big name and a big, big talent; he was such an elegant player and deadly around goal. When he arrived at Milan, though, he was still suffering the effects of a serious knee injury and had lost a little bit of his pace. But he had a positional sense which helped make up for that, and a touch on the ball which had to be seen to be believed. He had such happy feet and he was so good to play with. I learned a lot from being with him.

At Monaco I played with the Argentinian, Ramon Diaz, who had also been in Italy and who was just an out-and-out goal-getter. That's all that mattered to him. He didn't care about any of the other players in the team. I doubt if he even cared all that much about the team – just as long as he was getting his name on the score-sheet. He was easily the most selfish player I have ever known. But he was good at the job of snatching goals and, while he could annoy you, that was something you could never take away from him. He had all the tricks you expect from South American players, but off the ball he was lazy. He just would not work until the ball was at his feet. Then watch out – but don't ever expect a pass if he even had a glimpse of goal. He was a complete individualist and a lethal finisher, but there was never any way that he could have developed into a team player. That was simply something that did not cross his mind. Goals were all he cared about, and that possibly held him back as a player. As a youngster he was rated higher than Maradona in the Argentinian youth team, but it was the other fellow who made the world-class reputation. Again, though, Diaz was a finisher of the very highest class; maybe part of his problem was that he knew that better than anyone else and it took over his whole game.

When I kicked off my England career I was playing with Tony Woodcock and Trevor Francis, both of whom were just about winding up their careers at that level. I actually took over from Paul Mariner. Gary Lineker was the best I played with for England. He had such fabulous pace and he used it to such devastating effect. You didn't give him the ball the way you would give it to other strikers. It was no use letting him have it to his feet. He allowed the pass to beat the defender and then he would ghost in behind and hit the ball as he was moving clear of any challenge. Most of his goals were scored on the deck and most of them in the penalty-box where he was just deadly.

Coisty has that knack too, and he has added to it to become a better all-round player. I think that's why we have worked so well together. We have both been able to add to our game. When a partnership is allowed to develop over a long number of games, it should just get better and better, so long as the two of you are compatible to begin with. We were – it just took the club a little bit of time to find that out. Of course, the more games we have, the more we learn about each other. It becomes habit. You know where to look for each other and you know the kind of pass your playing partner likes – or doesn't like. We all develop little traits in our game and so you know what these are too and you adapt your own game, at times, to dovetail with your mate's. It all becomes second nature and, if you get it right, the end result is goals and more goals. So Coisty and I must have got it right over the last two seasons.

He would be in my all-time list of greats. He would be with Virdis and Rossi and Lineker and all the others and let's not have any criticism about him scoring goals in a lesser League. I won't have that. Our League in Scotland is as competitive as you can get anywhere. Besides, scoring goals is difficult in any League and at any level. No one lies down to let you get the amount of goals we have scored between us since we started working together. And we've nicked a few in Europe, too, when we were up against the cream of our profession. Ask anyone in England about the goals against Leeds. I guess that must have shut up a few big-mouths who like to take a pop at us with all the insults about the standards up in Scotland. My answer to them is: come up and try it. Then they would know the demands placed on players with Rangers. They are as high as you will get anywhere in the world.

CHAPTER THREE

Career Worries and an Ibrox Lifebelt

The worst period of my life was that long, long spell when I was out through injury. It is hard to explain to people who have not played the game, or even to players who have not had to fight back from injury, just how depressing it can all be – not only to yourself, but to your whole family.

I went through that at a period in my footballing career when I should have been lining up one fresh challenge after another. It was my second season with Monaco. My new contract had been signed. I was making more money than I ever dreamed of and we were playing in the European Cup. It was a first for me and as such it was one of the peaks of my career at that time. It was a good side at Monaco with a good coach, Arsene Wenger, who is still there, and both Glenn and myself felt that we had a chance to perhaps win the European Cup.

Then, in the second round of the competition, disaster struck. We were playing against the Turkish side Galatasaray when a long diagonal ball was played towards me. I came into the box for it and, as I did so, my foot stuck in a rut. My foot jammed and the ankle went. Then a tackle came in and knocked the foot back the other way and the damage was done – only, at the time, I didn't have the slightest idea of just how bad the injury would prove to be. There was no pain, so I played on until half-time and then had the physio take a look. That's when I got the first indication of how serious the damage was. I had been playing with the ankle taped up because I had had a problem or two before and the physio and doctor at the club reckoned a little extra support would be best for me until the injury cleared. So, in the dressing-room at half-time in that European Cup game, they had to remove the support before they could get a good look at what had happened to the ankle. It was not pretty . . .

What had happened, essentially, was that the strappings had held the ankle together. When they were taken off the whole thing just exploded. It ballooned enormously and my foot was left flapping around uselessly. I had not felt any pain for the awful reason that all the nerves in the area had been damaged. I sat with the foot in ice until the end of the game but, by then, the whole area was black and the doctor had decided that an operation had to be performed the next day. It was a case of rebuilding the ankle using carbon fibres and screws in an attempt to repair the damage which had been done to the ligaments and joints. They chose to work on one side of the ankle only, believing that the other side would repair itself.

Unfortunately, things didn't work out the way the surgeons had hoped. So, five months later, after trying to make some kind of comeback, I was back at the clinic in Lyon for another operation. The explanation was that there were too many bits and pieces floating around in the ankle to allow it to mend on its own. It was one of the top clinics in the whole of Europe and they did a brilliant job – my only complaint was that if they had done both sides at the same time, I would have been playing again that much sooner.

After that I started again trying to build up the ankle until it was strong enough to get me back into action. But I still had problems in training, though they told me there was nothing wrong and to keep on running and training and everything would be okay. They tried to tell me that it was all in my mind and that the mobility I was looking for in the joint would arrive soon enough. The trouble was that I was not able to get any real movement in the ankle and I was finding myself in a great deal of pain. I just couldn't turn properly and it began to get me down. These were days when I was wondering if there was going to be any way back for me.

Quite genuinely, you find yourself in the pit of despair when things are as bad as they were with me. It was then that my family and my mates helped me. Some nights I would just sit there getting drunk because I was beginning to think there was no future for me in football. I just got so depressed that it was difficult to handle. Having a few too many drinks on the worst nights was something of a release. And I would talk to my dad and he and my in-laws and mates would come over to see us or they would talk to me on the phone in a bid to help keep my spirits up. My dad always told me that when you had the support of the people around you, the people closest to you, then you didn't have to worry too much. My friends and family did help enormously but there must have been times when I tried their patience to the limits because there are those days when you are down, those days when you are feeling sorry for yourself, those days when you cannot see yourself ever being back in action. And when that first operation went wrong and I faced problems even after the surgeons operated for a second time, I hit rock bottom.

Sometimes, though, you need to go down that far before you hit the long, hard road back. That's how it turned out with me. I simply took matters into my own hands.

Against the coach's advice, against the physio's advice, against the surgeons' advice and against the club's wishes, I flew home to England to consult a specialist there. He saw what was wrong almost immediately. He performed the third operation which was needed and soon I was able to start the long slog back to full fitness. The doubts about my long-term future had been laid to rest.

It took hard work to get myself ready to play again – and it took determination as well. Being out for that length of time – and by now I'm talking almost a year of doubts and uncertainty – affects you psychologically as well as physically. You cannot help worrying over how you are going to be when you get back, and by the time you have reached the stage of *knowing* that you will return to playing the game, you have had months of worry about even reaching that stage.

There is no easy way round it all and I was not the first player to find that out. Nor will I be the last. It was the most frustrating period of my life and I know there were times when I behaved badly and only the patience of the people around me kept me going and gave me the reassurance I constantly needed.

Then, when I returned to the first team and began to feel that the future was still going to be a bright one for me in a football sense, injury struck me down again. I was just three matches into my comeback bid when I was out once more. We were playing a game against Marseille and were leading by two goals to nil – and I'd scored one of the goals. Ten minutes before half-time I jumped for the ball, came down okay, and then there was a clash and as I landed my leg was jammed beneath another player. More drama. More worry. And another operation. Then a return to the gym and the work of rebuilding the ankle again and restoring my confidence. Nothing was ever simple about these injuries. I didn't seem able to just pick up a strain or a pull, or torn ligaments, which would keep me out for four or five weeks. No, I had to get the type of injuries which required surgery, extensive treatment and four or five months out of football. This time the injury came around January and meant I was going to be out until the end of the season. That added up to almost two whole seasons out of the game, and not far off eighteen months with only a handful of games to remind me what my profession was.

It would now be heading towards the summer of 1990 before I knew I would be ready to play again. The World Cup – a tournament I had very much wanted to take part in again – was to be played in Italy. Some of the games would be only a few hours' drive away from Monaco. In a playing sense, though, they were a million miles away from Mark Hateley, and that was just another blow to add to all the others.

Sure, I still had a contract, a very lucrative contract and one which still had two years to run. But I felt my time was up at Monaco. I really did feel that it was time for a move. The problem was who would want me. It had to be someone with a long memory after all the time I had spent on operating tables, treatment tables and training grounds. Still, I was ready to take the gamble of making myself available if the club would agree to let me go.

I spoke to the coach, Arsene Wenger, explaining that I needed a change of environment. We sat down together and I tried to let him know how bad it had all been for me since we won the French title. He understood and was sympathetic. I told him that I had to try to resurrect my career and that, to do so, I thought it would be better to get a move away from the club and the bad memories it now held for me. I still had not played and he was aware of the risk I was taking, but I think he respected me for wanting to

43

do so. After all, I could have sat tight, knowing my money was still going to be there even if I never got back to top form in my remaining years at Monaco. So he told me that he would not try to talk me out of my decision to leave, nor would he be hard to deal with if a club came in with an offer for me. As far as he was concerned, I would be free to have signing talks and I would be allowed to move just as long as Monaco were to get a reasonable fee.

That was when Graeme Souness came in to throw me the Ibrox lifebelt. He had watched what had happened to me and now, when he ascertained that I was fit to play again, he swooped. While the rest of the football world was concentrating on the finals of Italia '90, Graeme was in Monaco, sitting down with me to hammer out a deal which would take me to Rangers. I signed this time, and he then told me what he wanted from me – which was exactly what I had been doing throughout my career. He wanted a target-man and he still believed that I was the player for the job even though I had seen my career so brutally interrupted by injuries. They didn't put Graeme off. I told him that I would be ready to play in the new season and that was good enough for him.

Obviously, before the deal was finalised, I had to go through a medical. The Rangers doctor took me to the hospital and my ankles were examined thoroughly. The doctors told me how good the work which had been done was, and within half an hour gave me the all-clear to continue my career as a Rangers player. It has been little more than a formality even though, beforehand, I had had a few butterflies about it. I had suffered so many disappointments that I didn't want to see this deal go sour on me at the last gasp. Deep down, though, I knew everything was fine. I knew the operations had all been carried out perfectly but, after those long, anxious months, I could not help but have a few little doubts thrusting their way into my mind. They were banished and I knew, as certainly as I had always known, that I was now on the road back.

I have always been a very determined sort of person, and I had this burning desire inside of me to hoist myself back to the level I had been at before the nightmare began. I wanted to achieve all that I had achieved before taking these ankle knocks. I wanted to be back at the top. Now, with my future settled, I began to channel all that natural determination into regaining full match fitness. I think that attitude is hereditary, something I got from my dad, who has the same streak in him. Basically, the secret is never to know when you are beaten, never to know when you should give up. That has always been part and parcel of my approach to the game – and now it became even more important to me. I still had a hunger to be the best and Graeme had shown enormous faith in me. It didn't matter to him the length of time I had been out. I think he saw in me a quality he had in abundance himself as a player, as a manager and as a person. He is no quitter and he recognised that I would not give up on anything either. It was a situation where others might have had doubts about me even after the medical gave me a fitness all-clear. Some people might have believed that I had earned so much money in Italy and in Monaco that my ambition had been blunted. Anyone thinking that doesn't know me. The money didn't enter into it when I came back to Rangers. I could have stayed happily in the Mediterranean sunshine and made 'loadsa money' without facing the same challenges which were waiting for me at Ibrox . . .

What I wanted were those challenges. I wanted to help Rangers become even more successful. I wanted to help them make a mark in Europe and carve out a reputation for the club on the Continent. I wanted to be a part of the revolution the club had already set in motion in Scottish football. And I wanted to be with a club where passion ruled the fans and where ambition ruled the players. I heard rumours about other clubs in England who might have been interested, but this time, I knew where I had to go. I had made no mistakes in the other major career moves when they had come around, and I knew that I was making no mistake this time either. I had a manager who believed in me and a club I, myself, believed in. What more could I want to end the hurt which had been with me for so long?

CHAPTER FOUR

England Expects . . .
But Not From Me

I got my first chance to play for my country when I was just twenty-two years old and still playing in the old Second Division with Portsmouth. My form in the Under-21 team, plus injuries to other main strikers, allowed me my chance back then . . .

Gary Lineker dropped out of the tour to South America with a groin injury. Paul Mariner was also ruled out because he was unfit, and Trevor Francis had been forced to play for Sampdoria in the Italian Cup. I was left as the one out-and-out front man in the touring party, and having helped the Under-21 side win the European Championship, I felt I was on my way.

Now, almost ten years down the line, any hopes of the England adventure continuing have gone. I'm convinced that I would have to be the only – and I mean *only* English striker around before the manager, Graham Taylor, would pick me. Since he took over the job he has made a habit of ignoring any claims I might have. And, to be blunt, before his crucial World Cup qualifying games against Poland at Wembley and Holland away from home, I had decided I did not want to play for him. There's just no point. Taylor picked me just once, for a friendly game in Prague against Czechoslovakia back in the spring of 1992, as the team were preparing for the finals of the European Championships in Sweden that summer. Looking back at that now I'm fairly sure that he decided to put me in the side because of pressure from the press and people in the game. There was a lobby for my inclusion, a growing one, and that was something which pleased me. The problem is that I think it seriously embarrassed Taylor. He didn't want me, and, when he did choose me for that one and only match, he didn't have a single conversation with me.

Now, that's something I've never encountered before and I hope never to encounter again. I mean, how can you play for someone who doesn't talk to you? And, equally from a manager's point of view, how can you hope to get your ideas across to a player if you won't sit down to have a chat with him? If it's possible then it's a style of man-management that I came across for the first and only time when I joined Graham Taylor's England set up.

In all the time he has been manager of England he has come to see me only once – and I wasn't even playing on the day he made the long journey up to Aberdeen. That was a nice bit of pre-match know-how too. All he had to do was lift a phone and ask our manager, Walter Smith, if I was fit or not, and he would have had the answer. It would have saved him having to come to Scotland even once. That day I was sitting behind him in the directors' box at Pittodrie. He looked over in my direction and gave me a nod, and that was the limit of our contact. On the trip to Prague, the only level of conversation I reached with him was when I eventually asked him to stop calling me Tony. During training he kept shouting 'Tony' at me and it got me down a little bit, so I pointed out my name and suggested we should get on with things because otherwise my old dad would be having more mentions than me for England. That stopped him dead in his tracks but it was also the only exchange we had on the whole trip. Hey, the previous manager, Bobby Robson, wasn't the best with names either and sometimes called me Tony – but he did speak to me as well, and when he sat down he usually got the name right.

When I joined the squad there was no real welcome the way there had been before for someone joining up as a new boy or, in my case, as an old boy returning to a much-changed squad. The lads were great but the manager said nothing. I felt very ill at ease, and really a bit uncomfortable from the moment I reported until it was time to get back to Glasgow and my club.

It came as no surprise to me that I was left out of the squad which went to the European Championships in Sweden. Certainly, I had been troubled by a back injury during the last couple of months of the season, but I had recovered in time to play in the Scottish Cup final and had managed to score one of the goals at Hampden which gave Rangers a 2–1 win over Airdrie. That was enough to confirm my fitness and end any doubts Taylor might have had over my back problem.

That sad summer for England, I watched the European games from a bar in Florida on satellite television with my old mate, Chrissy Waddle. He is another who has suffered under the Taylor régime, and we met up over there and never missed watching a match. The manager of the United States World Cup team, Bora Milutinovic, was there too and he used to join us to see the games and discuss what was going on. The main thing he could not understand was why we were sitting having a beer with him several thousand miles from the action while England were suffering a nightmare. We felt the same way actually, but it was encouraging for the pair of us to have someone with his background and credentials in world football wonder what was going on with England. He thought we should be playing. He made that very clear, and this was the opinion of the man who had made such an impact with Mexico in the 1986 finals when everyone had written off the host nation. And, dare I say it, he was also the man in charge of Costa Rica when they defeated Scotland in Genoa in the Italian finals in 1990. He is a thorough professional and he has shown that again with the way his United States team performed against England last summer.

The following season the bandwagon rolled for Chris Waddle and myself again. Chris was doing his bit for Sheffield Wednesday and I was helping Rangers in that unbeaten European Cup run. The press wanted us brought back into the squad. Other players said that we should be back in the frame for England's World Cup games. Top club managers and coaches were insisting that Taylor was wrong to ignore our claims. But the barrage of support for us didn't move him one little bit. Or, if it did, it made him go against picking us. He seemed to become more and more entrenched in his attitude.

To some extent, I think that I suffered because I was playing in Scotland. There are still some people south of the border who don't rate the Premier Division – they should just try playing in it for a week or two. But even that argument, lousy though it is, went out of the window during our European Cup run at Rangers. We were playing the best in Europe, the very best, and we were matching them all the way. The Danish champions, Lyngby, were beaten twice – and Denmark are reigning European champions as Graham Taylor knows to his cost. The English champions Leeds United were also beaten in the home and away ties of the second round – and that should have convinced him of the worth of the football being played by Rangers.

If all of that was not enough, we went off on an unbeaten run of six games against the champions of the CIS, the champions of Belgium and the champions of France. I don't think Graham Taylor came to see even one of these games – and that strikes me as absolutely incredible.

So perhaps we have to look for another reason and one which would include Chrissy Waddle – and that's the fact that we are both over thirty years of age and he might think that is knocking on a bit to be playing for your country. If that is the case then it's even more of a nonsense than dismissing Scottish club football.

My former team-mate at AC Milan, Franco Baresi, is a year or two older than I am – yet when he decided to quit international football last season the Italian team boss, Arrigo Sacchi, begged him to change his mind. And Italy are simply not the same team without Baresi at the back. There are other examples from all round the world. This out-moded idea that players are finished when they hit the thirty mark should be laid to rest for good in Britain, because it is simply not true. In my own case, I can still feel myself getting stronger and I reckon I'm as fit now as I was when I started off with Monaco after being sold by Milan. In fact, I always maintained that the two seasons I had out would have to be added to my career expectancy and that's still the way I look at things. It was no bonus at the time but, as the end of my time as a player comes closer, I can see that the couple of years spent sitting on the sidelines can now be used to my advantage.

Anyhow, after my non-speaking role in Prague I never had any great expectations that I would get a recall. I had the feeling back then that Taylor was bowing a little to public opinion, and that all the time he was supposed to be giving me my chance he was hoping that I would flop. That was the very distinct feeling I was left with during the few days I spent as a member of the squad. And that is not the way you should be feeling when you're playing for your country. That, plus the double snub over the European Championship finals and then when he ignored me while I was playing some of the best football of my life for Rangers in the European Cup, made up my mind for me.

At the start of this season, Walter Smith told me that England had asked about me, obviously with the clash against Poland in mind. Taylor's number two, Lawrie McMenemy, came up to see me in a pre-season match, and that had kicked off the speculation once more. Newcastle United boss, Kevin Keegan, went public too when he declared that I was the man to lead England. The fans seemed to think the same. Lots of my fellow professionals did, too, and so did a few top club bosses. But Taylor didn't. In any case, it was too late by then. I didn't have any feeling left for the man who was in charge of the international side.

I talked things over with my wife, Beverley, and my dad, and while to some extent initially they might have wanted me to go if I was chosen, they quickly saw my point of view. The way he had treated Gary Lineker had made a lasting impression on me. Gary is the type of man who never has a bad word to say about anyone. He was a perfect professional and yet, at the end of his career, Taylor substituted him in the game against Sweden. For me, watching in that bar in Florida, it was the act of a manager who did not care for his players. A man who did not have any feelings for people who had served him well over the years. More importantly, Gary Lineker was a player who had done it for England, not just once or twice, not even a dozen or so times, but regularly over a long international career. Yet there he was, humiliated in front of millions of football fans and millions of his own countrymen who were watching the game back home. I did not want to end up being treated that way – and that had to be on the cards because, for whatever reason, Taylor clearly thought less of me than he had of Gary. He had underlined that in the previous season when he seemed hellbent on picking anyone but me for the main front role in the international side.

I could have helped the cause, you know. In the European Cup I was coming up against top-class Continental defenders and they all still have that fear of putting their head into a challenge when a ball comes flying across their goal from the flanks. It's my kind of ball, the one I love to go for – and they just hate that. They can't defend properly against that tactic. If a ball is played into their box straight on, they're okay: they can see what they are being asked to do, they know where the challenge is coming from. When they have to look around to see where an opponent is making his run from, they get edgy. I know how to play against these guys – I spent years in Italy and France doing it. I have also spent some time with Rangers matching myself against the top club defenders and I have held my own with all of them. I would have done the same for England.

But I never did get the chance. Graham Taylor played Paul Warhurst in one of the games, a centre-half who is on record as saying that he doesn't like playing as a striker. When that was happening, I felt Taylor was dumping on me from a great height. It would have been the climax of my career to help England get to the finals in the States and to go there with them. The way I was playing and the way I am still playing – I could have done that. And in spite of my own personal disappointment I backed England all the way – I'm a patriot who always wants to see his own country do well. But I couldn't care less about Graham Taylor. He is a man who had success at Watford where he played those long balls all the time, and since then he has done very little. I just don't think he has the ability or the background or the feeling to be in charge of a national side. I know that I was better than all the players he tried in international after international, and that's not being big-headed. I was also scoring more goals than at any time in my life – but he didn't even bother to watch me. Most managers would see that as not doing their job properly. Taylor must have a working pattern which is all his own.

It annoys me now that I allowed it to spoil part of the past couple of seasons for me. I realise when I think about things that I didn't have to prove myself to Graham Taylor. All I had to do was continue to prove myself for my club. If he ignored me then there was nothing I could do about it. But I could say no if he ever had a change of heart. Actually, I think he knew I would give him a knock back and that's why he didn't risk picking me for the Poland game. I'd rather spend next summer lying on a beach somewhere than trying to tell the England manager what my first name is. For England I'd go and play the way I always play, with as much determination as I possess. For Taylor – forget it.

To be honest, I think England should forget him and put a new management structure in place as quickly as possible. I think the job is far too much for one man. Or even two men, as it is now. I think that ex-England players – and none of them too old – should be brought in to help run the side under a supremo who has a deep knowledge of the game and a real understanding of the way players think and the way they react both off and on the field.

For the lieutenants I would look no further than Bryan Robson of Manchester United, someone who has proved himself time and time again to be an inspirational figure for England. Bryan is respected as a professional and the current players would benefit from his experience and from the patriotism he would bring with him. That's essential baggage for Bryan wherever he goes. He could help look after the defenders and the men who would be in midfield.

Also for the midfield area, I would draft in Glenn Hoddle, my old team-mate at Monaco. Glenn is proving himself as a boss with Chelsea. His time at Swindon and now at Stamford Bridge have added to his unique talents and should not be squandered. They should be looked on as a national treasure and utilised for the good of the England team.

And then we have Kevin Keegan to aid the attackers and, again, you are looking at someone who made a superb contribution to the game as an England player and who is now proving himself all over again as a manager with Newcastle United.

These men should be seconded from their clubs when the international team is playing. And they should become a vital part of the back-room which could help make England great again. All they need is a charismatic figure to mould them together into a team to take on the world.

My choice for that job would be Terry Venables – and I don't care how controversial that appointment would be. What I'm talking about here, remember, is football. I'm not interested in any of the problems Terry Venables may have had or may be having in business. I think Terry has all the qualities that a manager of the England football team should have. He has an immense amount of respect from everyone in the game. He has been successful as a manager here at home and a success when he took on one of the biggest jobs in the game, bossing Barcelona. I can recall playing for Terry when he was in charge of the Under-21 team. He was a man you could talk to, and a man you listened to as well. There was real communication and you could recognise from the start that here was a man who *knew* the game inside out. He has had experience at club level here and abroad as well as being a top-class player himself. He is the ideal choice as far as I can see and I just know that given a strong team around him he could bring back glory days for England. He might well be the man to change the game in a tactical sense and bring us into line with the rest of the world.

I don't see the present régime doing anything at all other than playing in the traditional manner when some kind of change is long overdue. Terry Venables is the kind of manager who is receptive to change. He is not one of the diehards who would resist anything which would at long last have us in step with the other major footballing nations.

I'm mainly talking about the 'sweeper' system which in this country appears to make people cringe whenever it is mentioned. Yet the Italians use it and the Germans use it and the French use it – I could go on and on about the number of nations who play this way. In Britain it has a reputation for being a wholly defensive set up and that is just not true. When it is played properly it can be a very aggressive system. You have three players at the back and you push your full-backs forward into the midfield areas. When you have possession, you get people into attacking areas; when you lose the ball, you haul them back. I can remember when I was in Italy having the system described to me. I was told there that a team should blossom when it has the ball, and when you lose it, you retreat and you close up, the way a flower's petals shut when the rain comes. It's a perfect way to describe the set up.

Good players can adapt to any style of play, and, when you are at international level, you are talking about seriously good players. I know that we have the zonal system drummed into us and defenders are used to 'passing players on' but if we are to be a power in the game again then maybe we should look at the sweeper system. I know that Terry Venables and the players I have mentioned above would all know exactly how it works. And how well it can work. We can't go on just believing that because we're British and gave the game to the world that we are therefore right. Only something revolutionary can lift the game here back to the top. It's no use doing the same old things all the time. Yes, we do have attributes of our own that we can utilise. We have strength and running power and ability in the air. We close players down well in the middle of the park – and the Italians have not been slow in following up on that example. That's because they don't close their minds to the way the game might develop outside the Serie A. They go around the world and they take note and what they like, they use. What they don't like, they just ignore.

When you come to a system which is universally used outside these islands of ours, you have to take a hard look at *why* we don't adapt. Closed minds is my view – and if we had Terry and Glenn and Kevin and Bryan running things, we would not have that attitude any longer. We would have men who have been around on the Continent as players and as managers, and we would see the game take on a new shape.

I might not be a part of it but I would applaud any moves to change things from the sidelines. My time is probably over but I would like to see the England team progress, and I doubt if that will happen until there is a dramatic change at the top and in how the team is run.

We need that and we need that desperately. It would be nice to think that some of my old England team-mates could help bring about the revolution. In the meantime, I hope that England do well enough, just as I would want my country to do whether they were playing hockey or rugby or football. But if they do get some success, I have to admit that I would rather see it come to a much nicer man.

CHAPTER FIVE

The Champions' League and a Couple of Regrets

*Typical Hateley action as he challenges in the air despite being
surrounded by Hibs defenders*

Earlier goal celebrations with his first striking partner at Ibrox,
Mo Johnston

A familiar sight as Mark Hateley and Ally McCoist celebrate another goal for their prolific partnership

Paolo Rossi, one of the great striking partners Mark has had during his four-country career

Two Dunfermline defenders arrive too late to stop a Hateley thunderbolt heading for their goal

All the power and determination which have made Mark Hateley one of the most feared front-men in football are seen here as he moves past the former Hamilton defender, Jim Weir

Alex McLeish of Aberdeen is one of the defenders Hateley respects most in the Scottish game. Here are the two in a typical joust

A despairing challenge by a Marseille defender, but Hateley was there first in the Champions' League clash

One of the few bad moments Mark has suffered since joining Rangers: he is shown the red card during the Scottish Cup clash with Celtic at Parkhead. Pieter Huistra walks away as ref Andrew Waddell holds up the card

Mark Hateley goes down in this challenge from Hibs defender Gordon Hunter

Airdrie 'keeper John Martin just gets there to stop Mark's goal attempt in the Scottish Cup final. The Ibrox man had the last laugh when he scored later in the game to help his side to victory

Graeme Souness, the man who lured Hateley to Rangers with the promise of winners' medals

Archie Knox and Walter Smith with the League Championship trophy

A pensive Mark Hateley – could he be thinking over that move into defence for the later stages of his career?

My time with Rangers has thrown up so many highlights that it's very difficult for me to pick out which has been the major event of the past few years. Among the best memories would be the first Premier League title win I was a part of when it went right down to the wire and a last-day decider against Aberdeen . . . Or the day we beat the Scottish Cup jinx which had hung over the club for so many years with our defeat of Airdrie at Hampden . . . But I think all of the players at Ibrox would agree that the combination of events which saw us go through Europe unbeaten in the Continent's top tournament and our first-ever participation in the Champions' League format comes as high as any of the club's many achievements.

It was a glorious season, with the 'treble' of Premier League title, Scottish Cup and League Cup to celebrate at home and so much to rejoice over on the even bigger stage of Europe. And yet when I look back at the matches I have to admit to a couple of regrets over the way it all ended with us as runners-up to Marseille in our group.

The first regret is that Ally McCoist and myself were seen as a partnership in these crucial Group matches for just

225 minutes out of the six matches. In the two full matches we played together we took three points away from home – two of them against the team from Moscow CSKA, after beating them 1–0 in Bochum in Germany where they were forced to play their home match. The other came from our visit to Bruges where we drew 1–1 against the team who were champions of Belgium.

The other forty-five minutes was all I lasted against Bruges at home, and that's the second regret which still nags away at me. How I was ordered off in that match I will never understand properly. The player who was involved with me in that incident, right on half-time when we were winning 1–0, was their thirty-one-year-old defender, Rudi Cossey – there's a name I won't forget in a hurry, because of what he cost me and possibly Rangers. Before the first-leg game in Belgium he had been telling the fans over there just how he was going to match me physically and how he would be able to sort me out. Basically, that is defender-speak for kicking lumps out of the opposing centre-forward. On this occasion it just happened to be me. Over there it was not too bad, but at Ibrox, where Bruges were always going to be under the cosh, the pre-match threats had been repeated and this time round he was intent on following through during the match.

So, a few minutes after Ian Durrant had given us the lead, Cossey put me in what I can only describe as a headlock close to the halfway line as we both went for a high ball. I threw his arm off me – a natural reaction when someone has your head in their grip. That's all I did, just shoved him away to allow me to get on with the game. And then I was shown the red card. Not the yellow one, the red – and this without even having had a warning beforehand. I couldn't believe it then and I still find it hard to believe now. But the Polish referee had made his mind up and I knew there was no point in arguing. All that would have done would be to compound the offence, and that was the very last thing I needed. I'm still sure that if the authorities had been prepared to look at the evidence from television then I might have escaped suspension for at least one of the two remaining games, if not both. They would have seen that I was going for the ball when I shoved him off. I wasn't even looking at Cossey at all. What I wanted was to get clear of the grip he had on me and get on with the game. It was rated 'violent conduct' by the referee and by UEFA but it was never that. It was no more than an instinctive reaction made in the heat of the moment. I should have known better. With all my experience, I should have made sure that I got the free kick and he got the warning – but instead I tried to get on with the match and that turned out to be a big, big mistake.

I missed the game in Marseille when the team needed my presence there. And I was out of the last of the group games at Ibrox against CSKA when we knew that victory would be essential if we were to have any chance at all of reaching the final against AC Milan. They had stormed away as clear winners in the other group of four teams. No one could touch them – while, in our group, the qualification for the place in the final was balanced very finely until the closing games. In a way, they reached the kind of climax which UEFA had always hoped for in their new format.

The only lousy thing for me was that I had to be a very unhappy and very impatient and very bad-tempered spectator. It was not the best of times for me in a tournament which had been so important for the club and for all the players. Before we set off on the journey to the Champions' League and to the brink of a place in the European Cup final we knew, all of us knew, that the one barrier left for us as a team was to do well in Europe. We had ended the Scottish Cup jinx which had lasted eleven years. Now, after flopping so often in Europe, we had a chance to do something in *the* major club competition.

We had no illusions as to how very, very difficult our task would be, but we also knew that we were good enough as a team and as individual players to make an impact on the European Cup at last. We also recognised that we had to show ourselves capable of playing really well at the highest level at some time or another. Walter Smith knew that. So did his assistant, Archie Knox. And so did all of the players in the first-team squad. Personally, as well as our ability, I reckoned that we now had the experience and the character and the temperament to go further than we had been able to go before. Not that that was too hard – getting beyond the first round had proved difficult to us in previous years. To be fair, we had gone out to classy opposition. One year in the second round we fell victim to Red Star Belgrade who went on to beat Marseille on penalties in the final. Then, the previous season, we had lost at the first hurdle to Sparta Prague who had gone on to knock out Marseille before taking their place in the newly formed Champions' League.

I think that the fans knew, too, that the ties had been tough. But we had been desperately close to victory over the Czechs and more was expected from us as Scottish champions. Yet, when the draw was made, our luck looked as though it had been out once more.

Little more than a month before, Denmark had shocked the world of football by winning the European Champion- ships after being drafted in at the last moment to take over from the players of war-torn Yugoslavia, who had been disqualified by the UEFA on the eve of the tournament kicking off in Sweden. Now, when the draw was made in Switzerland for the first rounds of the three UEFA compe- titions, we found ourselves facing the team who were champions of Denmark, Lyngby. Not only was this club, based just outside the capital city of Copenhagen, formidable opposition in their own right, but we knew, as Walter Smith warned us, that they would be boosted by the summer success of their country. We won the first-leg game 2–0 at Ibrox, when I was able to score one of the goals and Pieter Huistra grabbed the other. Then, over there, Ian Durrant nicked one and we were through comfortably even though they had given us some worrying moments over the two legs.

I don't care which team you talk about here: when you are playing at the very highest level, the difference between success and failure is a narrow, narrow line. On that occasion we walked the tightrope safely and were into the second round even though, initially, we did not know who our opponents were going to be. The German champions, Stuttgart, in an unbelievable blunder, had played against Leeds United using one more foreign player than they were entitled to field in the game at Elland Road. They had won the first-round tie on aggregate but now UEFA had to act on the breaking of the rule governing foreign players. When they did so, they allowed Stuttgart to stay on – but only for a Barcelona play-off against the men from Elland Road. Leeds won that and so, when the dust had settled over that controversial Euro tie, we were left to face the prospect of lining up against the full might of the English First Division champions, who had denied Manchester United the title at the last moment in the previous season. From the minute it was known that the Battle of Britain was to take place, we were written off in England. The newspapers, the television and the radio, and the general public all forecast a Leeds victory – and when Gary McAllister gave them their spectacular start at Ibrox with that opening-minute goal, they must have sat back smugly saying 'We told you so'.

But we knew better because we knew that we had the guts to fight our way back into the game and the support to help carry us to victory. And that's how it turned out. Before the game I had said in the dressing-room that I honestly believed that we would win one match and draw the other and go through to the Champions' League. Most of the lads felt the same way – it was, after all, the tie we had wanted. When there were doubts and when the play-off in the Nou Camp stadium took place, we were all rooting for the Elland Road side to get through because we all wanted to have a crack at them. There was a strong element of the Scotland–England thing at work, of course. And even though I'm English I knew that the way the team was being written off before a ball was kicked would work to our advantage.

Having spent some time up here now I know how good the top Scottish teams are and how high the level of competition is. Okay, we have won the League six out of the last seven years, but there are other countries where the championship is dominated by just one or two clubs. Even down in England you would be able to name three or four sides at the start of each season and reasonably expect one of them to end up as champions. Last season some of the games we saw on the box from the new Premier League in England were lousy. We saw bad goalkeeping and poor defending, and yet people have the nerve to slag off Scottish football when they rarely see any of the teams in action and very few of the games even on television. If you examine what was played down there last season and then take a look at what went on in the Scottish Premier League, I doubt if you would be able to see very much of the so-called gap that English commentators always allege lies between the two countries. Yes, there is greater in-depth strength as you would expect from a much larger country. But if you examine the top teams here – ourselves, Aberdeen, Celtic, Dundee United, Hearts and Hibs – then you are seeing sides who would hold their own against most or all of the better teams down south. I wasn't surprised at that when I first arrived on the Scottish scene because I had watched some of those sides in action in Europe and I'd seen the level of competitiveness there was in their play.

The game in Scotland is a whole lot faster than it is anywhere else I've played. You don't get a minute to settle on the ball. There is no way that a midfielder has the chance to put his foot on the ball and slow things down. Try that and you get a very rude and very sudden awakening to what the game is about. I'm not saying that it is the best way to play the game – but it is the way it is played here and you have to adapt to it or else you won't be able to survive. It's fast, it's frantic, and it's furious and it's exciting.

The people who wrote us off should have known that. Even after the first-leg win – and I think we were playing for the whole of Scottish football that night as well as for ourselves – they were still at it. That's what allowed me to savour that goal of mine – the perfect reply to the strike from Gary McAllister in the first leg – more than normal. It surprised the Leeds fans and it surprised a few of their players too. I think they knew they were going to be facing a hard, hard night and that's how it turned out. We had always felt that we would score there. The management had preached that to us and we had known ourselves that because of the way we approach games in Europe we always have chances to get goals away from home. When we travelled south with a lead from the first leg, I knew that Coisty and I would find gaps among their defenders in the second leg. They were always going to leave space because they had to attack, and that meant their full-backs being thrown forward so that when we broke we could damage them.

That was shown when the first goal went in. I know it was an opportunist strike – but the gaps were there and no one closed me down when I took possession. That underlined to all of us that our pre-match thinking had been correct. If we needed confirmation, it arrived with the second goal after half-time.

It was a classic goal away from home in Europe, one which should be shown by coaches when they are trying to put across the idea of hitting on the break – and doing it correctly. It started with a ball out of our defence when we were under a little bit of pressure, and this time as we broke forward, gaps opened up all over the place. I had time to look up and pinpoint Coisty with the cross for him to score. It was a famous victory and it's one I was glad to be involved in because I know how much it meant to everyone at the club.

It was one up on the English – a strike for the whole of Scottish League football. It catapulted us into the Champions' League and allowed our supporters to be the first fans in Britain to see what was involved in the new set up in the European Cup. And it brought to an end some of the sneers about Rangers being nothing more than a very big fish in a very small pool up in Scotland. Any player who thinks that should travel north and take a look at an Old Firm game or a clash at Pittodrie with Aberdeen or even a battle at Broomfield when Airdrie were in the Premier League. Any one of them and half a dozen others would change their minds about the challenges we face week after week in our own domestic game. Every single match is a cup final and is played that way. We are the team the others have to topple, and every single club in the League wants to do just that. When they do, it's as if they have won a major trophy instead of just beating Rangers. But it's that edge which keeps us going. It's that constant threat from every single team in Scotland which makes sure that not a single player at Ibrox can sit back and rest on any laurels which may have been won along the way.

It's that intensity which hardened us for the European Champions' League campaign even though when we started off in our group it looked as if we had blown it almost before we had had a proper taste of the big time. Those first fifty-five minutes against Marseille at Ibrox in front of almost 42,000 fans were a big, big blow to our confidence and to our self-esteem. And yet, because of that, we dug deep to find qualities which were to serve us so magnificently for the rest of a cruelly demanding season. We found a collective heart and a passion which was to carry us through difficult and dangerous games and bring the club the hat-trick of trophies at home as well as a nail-biting end to our adventure in Europe.

I think it was the Bruges coach, Hugo Broos, who said later in the competition that Rangers were a team who could never be written off, a team who did not know the meaning of defeat even when it seemed to be staring us in the face. He was right, and time after time we were able to prove him right in that epic season. There is a belief which runs through the entire team. Up front we have confidence in the defenders and, I guess, they have faith in the front men to keep scoring goals. The spirit in the team is unbelievable. No one in the side is bigger than anyone else. There may be players with greater reputations than others, but when we are playing together that's put aside. When we were playing those games in Europe it was like eleven brothers out there on the park. Each player inspires the others and there is no star system – during a game the main thing in your mind is not to let any of your mates down. On and off the pitch, I have never known anything which even remotely approaches the feeling we have at the club. I don't doubt for an instant that helped us to our successes last season.

Every player in the side is ready to accept responsibility during a game. Good players will always do that; it's one of the marks of a quality player. Even when your marker is tight up against you and ready to kick you, you still take a pass, you still make yourself available for the ball. Teams must have been frightened to score against us last year – because when they did we hit right back at them.

Look at the Marseille game to start with. Their Croatian striker, Alen Boksic, scored after half an hour and then Rudi Voeller, the German front-man, gave them a two-goal lead in the fifty-fifth minute. We were on the ropes. They must have thought that we were down and out. But we came back. Gary McSwegan came off the bench to hit the first goal within a couple of minutes of taking over from Trevor Steven and then, with eight minutes left, I snatched the equaliser. If the game had lasted another five minutes, I reckon we could have won it.

That's honestly how much of a turn-around there was. I was pleased at that result, pleased because of the way we had battled back into the game and pleased too, that we had stopped some of the mouth music which had been coming out of Marseille when they knew they were to play us in the first of the group games. Their hard-man centre-half, Basile Boli, had been saying how he was going to sort me out – and he wasn't able to do that. But I always feel when players start mouthing about what they are going to do then it's a dead giveaway that they are a lot more worried about you than you are about them. I've no doubt Boli meant all he said – I'd come up against him before in France, after all, and had the bruises to prove that – but I still felt I had the edge psychologically over him for that match. Basically, he had set out to intimidate me and he failed.

I only wish Coisty had been alongside me that night because I think we could have done even better. We didn't start playing until we were two goals down and, as well as being without Alastair, Richard Gough had been forced out of the match after just forty-six minutes with an injury. The toll of injuries never reached the proportions it did at the start of this season, but when you look back at the European Cup games you realise how often we had to go into important matches without key players. Our critics say we carried luck in the games. If we did, we sure as hell earned it with the blows we had to overcome almost constantly.

In our next match in Germany against the Russians we won 1–0 with Ian Ferguson getting an early goal for us. Coisty and I were together for that game but Richard Gough was still missing. That was an important result for us – a victory away from home which ensured that we would be chasing Marseille. It made up a little bit for the failure to win our opening home game and it was so inspiring the way the fans followed us to that little town in Germany, Bochum, where the game was played. They took over the place and they did the same when we went to Bruges three months later for our third game following the Euro winter break. Thousands of supporters were there and, again, they saw us go behind just a minute before half-time. Just as we had done before, though, they saw us storm back in the second half on their ground.

Goughie was missing again, as was Trevor Steven, but in the end Bruges were the team who were happy to hear the final whistle. Pieter Huistra scored our equaliser but their 'keeper had to make save after save after save, from myself, from big Dave McPherson, from Stuart McCall – he was incredible. On another night I think we would have won. What happened was that we found a goalkeeper in special form – and when you get that life can be very difficult. Still, we did earn another point and, with Marseille only drawing with CSKA in Berlin (a game they came close to losing in the dying minutes), we had stepped up our challenge to the French side.

Two weeks later Bruges came to Ibrox. I was sent off as I have already pointed out, we lost a goal soon after half-time and then Scott Nisbet – Nissy, bless him – scored an astonishing winner. It was no less than the lads deserved after my sending off and they had had to play with just ten men. Now it was a showdown with Marseille in the Stade Velodrome, a ground always rated as the most intimidating in all of France.

I was out through suspension for that game, and on a visit to Monaco before the lads played in Marseille, I began to hear the rumours which later surfaced so dramatically when the French side were stripped of the European Cup and their French title. The Russians, after their close-run match in Berlin, had crashed to a six-goal defeat in Marseille and rumours had spread like wildfire . . .

The Russians were claiming that they had been drugged, that their food in the hotel had been tampered with. The accusations, at that time, were not being made in public. But in France the stories were known to everyone in football. They reached me when I was in Monaco and they had also reached Ibrox. Walter Smith and the backroom staff took very serious precautions for that trip. We were staying in one of the best hotels in the South of France and yet we brought our own food, our own drinking water and our own chefs to make absolutely certain that no one could get near the food the players were eating.

I believe there was a serious worry at the club over the Russian allegations. It's a fairly normal procedure for a club to take food on trips to Eastern Europe or even on other trips closer to home – but in a country which prides itself on its food and its cooking, it was strange to see a team arrive with enough hampers to cater for every meal the lads took during their stay there. I never discussed the matter with Walter but I'm sure that these precautions were taken in case the CSKA accusations had some foundation. I mean, how could the scores be turned around in such a way inside a fortnight? The Russian team was more or less the same for the two games – with a notable addition to the side being the return of their number-one 'keeper who had been missing in Germany. It was a result which had eyebrows raised all across Europe. When the CSKA manager, Gennadi Kostilev, went public in the wake of the bribery allegations which hit Marseille over some of their domestic games, the care the club took over our own visit to France was a sensible precaution. The Russians were insistent that something had happened to several of their players in the hotel before the game. Walter simply took no chances that anything could happen to us.

When I played for Monaco there were always rumours flying around, always gossip about the goings on at the Marseille club, but in the main I put it down to jealousy over their high-profile president, Bernard Tapie. He was involved in so many things – politics and football – in addition to his business interests. He was controversial, flamboyant and ambitious – the kind of man who would make enemies easily. So, while gossip circulated, I paid little attention to it. Now, though, the club is in crisis and stories about the methods used to gain success have been substantiated.

Rangers avoided controversy there – and kept the dreams of a European Cup final place alive even though I had to sit that one out.

I was not surprised by the result in Marseille. The Velodrome was always a good hunting ground for me when I played there with Monaco and that was why I was so upset at missing out on the game. I still think that if Coisty and I had been able to play together against the French side, we would have been in the final instead of them. We didn't go in against them together because Alastair was injured for the first match and I was suspended for the second. And I just knew we would score there because their defence was vulnerable. Durranty scored at their place after Franck Sauzee had given them the opening goal. Again, we fought back and, again, we might have snatched a victory.

They were very nervous, something which did not surprise me greatly. The atmosphere at their ground can sometimes work against them. The expectations of the support, built up by the president, are huge, and the demands on the players to provide success are fierce. That has them under pressure before a ball is even kicked in many of their really big games. It was a boost for us, a blow to them, but somehow I felt that they would get the win they needed in Belgium.

Don't ask me why, but I was left feeling that one win over them, just one in the two games, would have been what we required to make sure of a clash with Milan in the Olympic Stadium in Munich. It would have been a dream game for me going in against my old team and getting the chance to settle an old score with their president, Berlusconi. But it was not to be. They *did* win in Bruges and we dropped a point at home to CSKA and the adventure was over.

It was a marvellously emotional night at Ibrox even though we did go out. More than 43,000 fans were there and at the end, while grown men wept in the stands, they stood and cheered the team. They were not going to Munich but they still stayed on long after the final whistle to pay tribute to the lads and to say 'Thank you' to us for our efforts. It made the disappointment a little easier to bear because we knew that we had kept a dream alive for these supporters all through the season. Now, we knew, we had to deliver the 'treble' to make the season a truly memorable one.

We did that, history was made, and we still had an unbeaten European Cup record to console us. It was hard to accept when the news of the Marseille problems hit the front pages. But I was never in favour of the final being re-staged between Milan and ourselves. I did not think that was the answer and I'm glad that UEFA did not adopt that course of action. It would not have done anything for the image of the game. The Cup winners have been punished and that is surely enough. Anyhow, we still have our memories and nothing can take them away from any of the lads who played in these matches.

CHAPTER SIX

That Old Gang of Mine

The public must know by now how I feel about Rangers as a club and as a team. I've never been with a better group of lads than the squad of players we have at Ibrox, and I genuinely believe that Rangers, as a club, are now among the élite of European football. Sure, we'll have setbacks like the one we suffered in Sofia when our old first-round European Cup jinx returned to mug us so soon after that unbeaten run the season before. But the club – and the players – are strong enough to overcome any disappointments we may have.

In some ways I would say Rangers are an even bigger concern than AC Milan. For a start, Rangers own their stadium and it is one of the finest in Europe. Milan don't: the San Siro is municipally owned and they share it with Inter Milan. To counter that, Milan have their own training ground which we don't yet have . . . but I still think the Rangers way is right. Ibrox is a magnificent asset and because it is owned by the club, corporate hospitality is on offer all through the week as well as on match days. Milan have nothing to compare to that. Nor do they have the boxes which can generate so much money for Rangers.

There is a different approach, but there are things which each club has in common. Both have highly ambitious men at the top, for example. David Murray, who is the chairman of Rangers, and Silvio Berlusconi, the president of Milan, are both wealthy men with business track-records in their own countries which they have adapted to the successful running of top football clubs. This is without any doubt the way ahead for the game. Top businessmen can make things happen in a way that the old school of football directors could never do. They are so much more alive to commercial opportunities, to sponsorship deals and to promotions than other, older directors could ever be. I think you will find, in the very near future, clubs being run by a chairman and a manager the way it is done in so many places on the Continent. Weekly board meetings are a part of yesterday's game. It is surely much easier and much more efficient for the two main men at a club to sit down together and make policy decisions regarding the buying and selling of players and the direction the club is heading. I'm sure that's what happens at Ibrox. And I know that is what happens at Milan. Berlusconi talks to Fabio Capello and then things happen. There is, of course, a major difference between David Murray and Berlusconi: at Ibrox, Walter makes the team decisions while at Milan, as I know to my cost, Berlusconi interferes in the playing side of the club.

I suppose I always knew that Rangers were a big club. Even as a kid at school in England you would recognise that in Scotland Rangers were exceptionally powerful and they were able to make their mark in Europe, too. But it was only when I arrived at Ibrox that I realised just *how big* they are, and how much bigger they are than any of the other clubs in the country. Even when you bring England into the picture, the only club I can think of that could come near to matching us is Manchester United. It's hard for me to give a proper assessment of the two clubs, firstly because I'm obviously very biased, and secondly because I have not visited Old Trafford for some time.

But I do know that we have got things right here. The way things have developed over the past few years proves that. The stadium was magnificent when I got here, but now it's even better and there is still more work to be done. The chairman is a perfectionist and that's why Ibrox will be a showpiece and a stadium which is certain to host a major European final before too long. What would be special is for us to win another Continental trophy and to have a replica sitting there in the Trophy Room for all the world to see. It won't be this year – but I still think we can do it because of the attitude among the players and the self-belief which exists.

Everyone motivates everyone else. There's a lot of shouting out there on the park, plenty of encouragement, and some moans thrown in, too. But anything that is said during games among the players is said for the benefit of the team. If someone is having a bad game, a real nightmare, then the others simply buckle down that bit more and make up for it. If you are the player suffering then you know that there are ten others who are going to pull you through. Players are not detached from each other the way they can be at some clubs. We talk together as we work together and that's how we are all on the same wavelength when it comes to playing this great game of football. That is part of our secret.

There is another important ingredient: no prima donnas are allowed. Anyone who does try that on is brought down to earth with a bump, and no time is lost in making sure that's done. That's why, when you look at other top club sides, you start talking about the individual players. At Milan you talk about Jean-Pierre Papin and Marco van

Basten, or the other Dutch stars when they were there, Ruud Gullitt and Frank Rijkaard. At Marseille it was mainly about Boksic and Voeller and Abedi Pele. At Rangers people talked about us as a team and that's why we were so hard to beat. We operated as a unit. We fought together and we bled together and we worked our butts off for each other, for Rangers and the fans.

The club seems to be structured in such a way that every single person matters, from the chairman at the top right through the management staff, the players, the people who work in and around Ibrox and last, but certainly not least, the fans. Things are initiated at the top, run all the way down through this structure and then return via the fans who have their own views on what might be happening. We can have bad times and the supporters stay with us. Sure, they can dish out a bit of stick but there are times when every team and every player can deserve that. But when it reaches the crunch, the fans are with us. It's a bonus for the lads, knowing they have that to fall back on. We all needed the help and the support from the fans during the tough games we faced and during the few tough times when we were suffering a little . . . and they didn't let us down.

And I don't think we let them down too often either. Personally, I have almost never felt let down by the squad of players which has been put together at Ibrox – the squad which went through Europe undefeated. It is always, as I say, about the *team* first and foremost – but you cannot underestimate the quality of the players who are part of the Ibrox set-up. Let's take a look at them now.

Andy Goram was in goal then and we have missed him since he has been injured. That's no reflection on Ally Maxwell at all – in fact, he has said how it's a near impossible task taking over from Andy. Goram rammed all the jibes from all those years of criticism from English commentators back down their throats with his performances. He is brave and strong and has an air of confidence about him which spreads through the defence. He is quite an exceptional 'keeper. Some critics have commented on his lack of height, but he makes up for that by his sheer aggressiveness. When he comes out for a ball, it's always going to be *his* ball. He doesn't let anyone get in his way.

In defence for most of the games we have Dave McPherson at right-back, because Gary Stevens was injured. He might have been out of position but the big man did so well, and in the centre of defence he was magnificent in the air. I know how good he can be in that department because I had a few brushes with him when he was playing for Hearts. I'm glad he joined up again at Ibrox – it took away one of the difficult opponents.

Richard Gough could walk into any team in the world – apart from the Scotland international team, that is – because he is simply one of the best markers in the game. I've played against top defenders all over the world and I think I know what I am talking about. Goughie's organisational ability and his tackling and strength in the air, allied to his pace and positional sense, make him world-class.

For most of the matches he had John Brown alongside him. 'Bomber', the quiet man, is the one player in the squad who has never been capped. I don't know why, because if I was picking the Scotland team, he would be one of the first names down on the list. I would include him in any team because he is utterly dependable. Even after all the wear and tear he has suffered through injury, he is a player who never lets the team down.

David Robertson is still developing but he has the pace and running power that a modern full-back needs. He was outstanding last season and he is going to get better and better. It's frightening to think how good he can become.

Of course, for most of the season, my old English team-mate, Gary Stevens, was injured but he remains one of the best full-backs in Britain. His athleticism put him into that position years ago and he has remained there as far as I'm concerned.

Trevor Steven is another class act. Like myself, he was a player Graeme Souness pursued for several seasons before finally being able to sign him. He left for one season in that £5 million deal which took him to Marseille and somehow did not fit in there. That was no reflection on his ability, though. I think it was more of a reflection on what goes on at that club. It's a strange place and Trevor could have been the victim of some political in-fighting there. It was a massive bonus for Rangers to get him back. He has great touch and vision, which is why he remains in the England plans. I must ask him about Graham Taylor some time . . .

Stuart McCall is the dynamo of the side no matter what position he plays in. There is not a team in the world who would not like to have someone with Stuart's energy and ability. He will run and run and run, and I know that Italian teams would love him. I don't know how he does it. He has the best engine I've ever known in any player. The teams from the Continent used to look at him buzzing around and wonder how he could keep going. We wonder, at times, too. He is incredible.

Then we have Ian Durrant, our equivalent of Paul Gascoigne – and I mean that in the best possible way – in the playing sense. He can make those dangerous runs off the ball into positions where defenders just don't pick him up, the way Gazza does. He possesses uncanny anticipation and the ability to drift into areas which pose real problems for defenders. If he had not suffered that terrible injury, I think everyone in world soccer would be talking about Durranty right now. He has the potential to be that good, and the way he has forced himself back to the top after the injury nightmare shows that he has courage and determination to add to his skills.

Also in the middle of the park we have Ian Ferguson who, apart from being good enough to get into most clubs, would surely be able to *moan* his way into whatever team he wanted to play for. He is quite unbelievable the way he goes on – but on the field we are not seeing the player Rangers bought. He too has been plagued by off-the-field problems – not just injuries but, even worse, illnesses. He went down with hepatitis and tonsilitis and these are the kind of problems which drain away your strength and the effects linger on long after the illness seems to have cleared up. Poor Fergie has had years of that kind of thing to contend with. Now he is back, looking good – but still moaning – and I'll make a prediction about him right now: by the end of this season every major club in Europe will be wanting to buy Fergie. He is the aggressive modern-style midfield man that every team needs. Rangers are lucky to have him – and to know he will never want to leave. He's a Rangers fan as well as a Rangers player, remember. We have to remember that because if we don't, you can be sure there'll be another burst of moans from him.

After that we have Coisty and I have dealt at length with Alastair in a previous chapter. What more can I say than he's the best finisher I've played with . . . though I could add that he is now playing with the kind of partner he has always needed. And that takes care of my own Ibrox credentials.

We can't forget the skills of Pieter Huistra – or that goal he scored in Bruges – or the talents of Alexei Mikhailichenko. Then there were the youngsters: Neil Murray and Steven Pressley came in to play in top matches and in the years ahead they will realise just how much they learned from their early involvement.

TOP MARK!

I didn't have that chance – I went more or less straight from the English Second Division into the pressure pot of Italian soccer at the top level. And I loved every minute of it until politics at Milan saw me forced to leave . . .

CHAPTER SEVEN

Memories of Milan

There is little doubt that most people in football thought I had made a serious career mistake when I agreed to join Portsmouth from Coventry instead of looking towards a First Division side. But Bobby Campbell, the manager there, worked with me and made me a better player. He was also responsible, I suppose, for my dream move to Milan. He hammered more and more aggression into my play, which paid off with twenty-five goals that season for the club, even though the dream of promotion died . . .

But while the club's hopes perished, my own ambitions were still growing. The England Under-21 team gave me a platform – and so, later, did the full international team. Neither of these would have been available if I had remained with Coventry. I suppose a match at Hillsborough against the French Under-21 side started the whole crazy Italian business. I scored four goals in our 6–1 win, and in the second leg of this European Championship quarter-final my form held and I scored the only goal of the game over in France. In the semi-final I didn't play in the first leg against Italy but did play in Florence in a 1–0 defeat but we went through to an appearance in the two-legged final against

Spain. I managed to help myself to another goal in the final in our home game at Bramall Lane and that brought me sudden promotion to the full England side.

Weeks later I was on the plane for Brazil and the opening game of England's three-match South American tour which was in preparation for the World Cup in Mexico two years later. It was in the Maracana that I made my début for England and the goal I scored won the attention of AC Milan. Before I returned home a deal was being set up to take me to Italy. It was hard for me to accept what was happening. Milan had been linked with every top striker in Europe – and in South America, too – Rudi Voeller from Germany, Gomes from Portugal and Renato from Brazil had been listed as targets. Until that goal against Brazil they had not even heard of Mark Hateley of Portsmouth. But, once they had, and with the Italian signing deadline looming and their fans demanding action, Milan's general manager, Antonio Cardillo, and the president, Giuseppe Farina, moved into top gear. By the end of the most incredible month of my whole life I was going to Italy and to one of the biggest clubs in that soccer-crazy country.

My first knowledge of what was going on came from my new England team-mate, Ray Wilkins. He had been sold to Milan several months earlier for £1.5 million, although he did finish that season with Manchester United. Now he called me soon after we were back from the tour and told me that I had been recommended to Milan and that they had phoned him to ask about me. He explained that they had seen the goal I scored against Brazil on television and that was the start of their interest. Now they wanted to follow through.

It was all very hard to grasp. I was just twenty-two years old and here I was being talked about suddenly as a million pounds' target for one of the best-known clubs in the world. It was all like some crazy, crazy dream, but because the Italian clubs could not sign anyone after 28 June everything went into overdrive and I think I stayed in a state of some confusion throughout the often complicated negotiations. I had two years of my Portsmouth deal left and I had been happy with the contract they had given me the previous summer. It was a basic salary of £25,000 a year – and now we were talking about a basic salary of ten times that, with win bonuses on top. This was life in football's fastest lane – the Serie A.

Portsmouth soon agreed their deal, with the chairman, John Deacon, in charge of that part of the business. He was looking at a profit of something close to £800,000 after having me for just one year. Good business for a Second Division side – good business, in fact, for any side in the country. My own deal had to be settled, too, and that took longer. But eventually they were settled too and I flew to Milan the following day to discover at first-hand the kind of madness which surrounds football in Italy. Thousands of fans turned out to give me a welcome and the streets around the club offices were jammed. There were moments, then, that I began to wonder what I had let myself in for. Luckily my friend and agent, Dennis Roach, knew of the minefields ahead and guided me through them.

But Ray Wilkins was there and that was important. I was just twenty-two years old and having someone beside me with experience and a deeper knowledge of the off-the-field problems you can find was invaluable. I do believe that it is important to have someone with you from your own country in any case. It helps to know that you can talk to a team-mate, and you relate better to someone who comes from your own type of football background. Getting to grips with a different environment is not easy when you are not allowed a great deal of time to do so. Milan were not paying out a million quid and huge wages without expecting some goals from me immediately I went into action.

I think that is always something you have to realise about the game in Italy. It's too glib, too trite just to talk about the massive rewards that are available for the players. It is true that they pay a lot of money to the top players over there – but they expect a lot in return. That's the way it should be, too. But adjusting to the demands made on players is another matter when you first arrive. I was pitched straight into that new life – three weeks in a training camp where the staff worked us as hard as I've ever been worked anywhere. Morning and evening we were running, seriously running, for two or three hours at a time, with only a couple of hours off for lunch and a little bit of rest after eating.

The coach at Milan, Nils Liedholm, had just joined the club, too. He had had a run of great success with Roma, winning the title and the Italian Cup there and taking them to the European Cup final when they lost on penalties to Liverpool. While Farina, the president, was the person who seemed to be responsible for signing me, I was encouraged when I heard that Liedholm had announced that he approved of the signing and said that Milan needed a big, powerful striker. That was another little worry removed because, unlike Britain where the manager buys the players, in Italy it's often the directors who go out to buy the star names and the coaches are left to fit them into whatever team pattern can be worked out. This time, though, the one-time Swedish international striker was happy at my arrival, and that is encouragement in itself.

I managed to repay him in the first couple of training games we had against local sides from the area where we were preparing for the season. We won those games pretty easily I can remember, and I got a couple of goals in each. The most encouraging thing was that the other players in the team were responding to me being in the middle and they were hitting in the kind of cross balls I love.

*Just before he is ordered off Hateley walks away from Bruges hard man,
Rudi Cossey, who is on the ground*

*Hateley signals triumph here as he and Ian Durrant congratulate
Stuart McCall after another Rangers goal*

Young Stephen Wright is the Aberdeen player here who is beaten by Hateley in this clash

Talking things over with the gaffer – here Mark puts over a point to Rangers boss, Walter Smith

Hateley wins again and the stranded 'keeper is Dundee United's Alan Main

'Take a knock, give a knock,' says Hateley, and here he has taken one from Hearts defender, Craig Levein

Gotcha! Dundee United's Jim McInally laughingly owns up as he holds Hateley down in a Tannadice clash between the two sides

Another clash – this time with Hibs' Murdo Macleod, who is now boss of Dumbarton

Hateley arrives at Ibrox at last. Here he is welcomed by the club's then boss Graeme Souness, Mo Johnston and skipper Richard Gough

*A not so happy fella is Ally McCoist as he lets fly in this picture –
Hateley says that McCoist would hold his own with any club in
the world*

Young Hearts star, Alan McLaren, arrives on the scene too late as Hateley rams a header into goal

Rangers chairman, David Murray, like Berlusconi, bought a major club. Unlike the Milan president, though, Murray does not interfere with playing matters, says Hateley

But nothing ever goes 100 per cent smoothly and I was then sent off in my first match at the San Siro. It was against Brescia in another friendly and it was my first real taste of what goes on in Italian football. Forwards are always under threat – or they were back when I started to play for Milan. Defenders were sent out to stop you and referees seemed to think I was big enough to look after myself. So while I was turned into Brescia's target for the day, the referee didn't afford me too much protection. Eventually I turned to remonstrate with one of the worst offenders and he just went down in a heap. I was sent off.

The fans didn't mind. I think most of them enjoyed it even, but I knew I'd made a bloomer. I hadn't touched the lad but he made it look as if I had butted him. It was in the very last minute of the game so I didn't leave the team short for half a match or anything, but the next day I was hauled in front of Gianni Rivera, a one-time Milan player who was now one of the directors. He told me that I would have to adjust to the Italian game, that defenders went out of their way to provoke you. He was talking from a lot of experience so I listened, and when Ray also gave me a bit of a talking to I took the advice on board.

There has been a bit of a revolution over the past few seasons when attacking play has returned, but when I was there defences still ruled. Now when you look at the matches in Serie A it is so different. Their game is much more attack-minded than it used to be, much more aggressive than it was during my seasons with Milan. I'm not talking about tackling or challenges or people clattering into forwards. I'm talking about the kind of passes which you see being made. They are passes which open up play, which give scoring chances for front players that I didn't see with anything like as much frequency.

Back then, it was the slow, patient build-up, with the ball being passed among the back four until they could see a possible gap opening up. Then, and only then, would they release the ball. Now they try to *make* that opening appear. I'll tell you now there is no way they would ever have thrown the ball into the opposing penalty-box the way they do today during my spell there. And I genuinely believe that Milan really kick-started that revolution – one that now extends to the national side.

For decades, the Italians at club and at national level were looked on as the high priests of defensive football. Their credo was simple – 'Don't lose a goal and you won't lose the game'. I suffered because of that. It was frustrating for me even though I did find it all a part of a learning process. It was difficult, though, to adjust completely. In the beginning, in particular, I found it hard because the game I was being asked to play was alien to what I enjoyed and what I was good at. I was stuck up front, and unless the ball came to me, I was left there withering for ninety minutes. You could go a couple of games over there without getting a touch of the ball. The influence of *attanaccio* still hung over the game. The system which was used by Inter Milan under their boss, Helenio Herrera, had brought the team success at home and in European competition, and so most other sides copied that style of play. It was a killer for me.

I'm the kind of player who wants to be involved at all times in the game. Getting so little of the ball and so few goal chances was hard to accept, and my youth and lack of experience made me impatient. And while things had worked okay in the friendly games, when it came to the crunch the other players in the team were not always able to provide the service I needed. It was an adjustment they were being asked to make because they were not used to having a player such as myself in the side. So they were not playing to my strengths and they were not getting the ball into the box often enough or quickly enough. To be absolutely fair to the Milan lads, it would have been the same no matter which team in Italy I had joined. They just didn't play balls into the box the way I expected. It was a different kind of game for them and for me, and we both took time to feel our way through the new approaches which were needed before we could play together as potently as we knew Milan required us to do.

And yet while it was occasionally a miserable time for me, there was a chance to learn and to expand my playing range, and I was lucky that Nils Liedholm was my gaffer there. He had played as a striker himself and, along with his Swedish countryman, Gunner Nordahl, had built a reputation on the field which continued into coaching.

But it wasn't just that he had played in the same area of the field which helped me – it was also that he had been a foreign player who had had to adjust to the different lifestyle as well as the changing football environment which I was now trying to come to terms with. His own experiences more than twenty-five years earlier gave him an insight into my problems that an Italian-born coach could never have had. That helped me enormously.

In a football sense, too, he had an understanding of how hard it was to come into the kind of game where you were less involved than you had been before. He grafted new things on to my basic style. He taught me and encouraged me to be lighter on my feet. He told me that he had been surprised by the skills I possessed when the ball was on the ground – he had expected someone who was good in the air but who could do little else when given the ball. So he told me to be more comfortable with the ball at my feet. He said that I should appreciate the ball more because I was going to see so much less of it in Italian football. He wanted me to take a ball on the ground and *keep* it rather than knock it on straight away. He worked at making sure my first touch was improved so I could get the ball under control and keep it close and then make a pass or try a shot. He was able to recognise that I score more goals with my feet than with my head. I wonder how many people reading this book knew that? It's true, you know. People never reckon that. They just think that because you are over six feet tall you're just another big, ugly centre-forward – and old-fashioned too. But there has always been more to my game than that. My dad used to encourage me to play upstairs and downstairs and that's what I've always tried to do.

Liedholm was also against my chasing around after opposition players. He didn't see the value of an attacker charging back into defence and away from the area in which he is a danger. He used to tell me to use all my energy, all my running, within the width of the penalty box. He stopped me running out to the wings and he told me he wanted me to work that area of the field all the way from the halfway line forward to the opposition goal. His view was that he had other players to operate in the other areas of the field. He stressed all the time that mine was a specialist role and I have to save myself for that. It sounds so simple – but try to get coaches in other countries to follow that basic philosophy and you will run into problems. In England, for example, most managers would go crazy if you told them you weren't chasing back into defence because you have to 'save yourself' for scoring goals. They would axe you straight away. Your feet would not touch the ground.

But Liedholm was different. He knew what he wanted from me and he also worked out the best way to get that. He made it plain that it was a waste of my energy to go running back into my own half to help defenders when I was more dangerous staying upfield. He thought I was just dissipating my running power when I should be hoarding it and waiting for the attacking break to come our way. He believed strongly that strikers needed all their energy for inside the penalty box – and he didn't want me to leave that central area of the field for any reason at all. That's where I could do most damage – so that's where I had to stay.

He also taught me that I had to make the most of the goal chances I had. They were so few and far between that you could not afford to miss them. When you were managing to scrape together just two or three chances in a month of matches you can understand that if you muffed one, it was a long, long time before you had the opportunity to make amends to your team-mates and to the fans. I was lucky in that I was able to score fairly regularly – including one in my League début against Udinese at the San Siro and another in my first Milan derby when we managed to defeat Inter 2–1. That was an important one and I loved scoring it . . .

It was the first victory AC had had over their city rivals for eight years and the president, Farina, was delighted with me – which was quite a change because we had already had our differences. The deal which had brought me to Milan included a house and a car provided by the club and a certain number of air flights home for myself and the family. It was all down there in black and white, but Farina kept stalling on the house. Both Ray and myself felt we were being messed about and decided on a showdown. It took place at the club offices and we tried to explain our problems. Family life in a hotel was no use, and it was adding strain to both of our lives away from the club. It was just hopeless for our wives especially, as we were away from home so often at Milanello, the training camp, or alternatively away even longer when we were playing a match in another Italian city.

They didn't seem to understand and the meeting ended with me having a real shout-up with Farina as Ray tried to calm me down. He wasn't too successful, because I literally threw the book at Farina. He had handed me a book on the history of AC Milan, trying to make the point, I suppose, that we should just be happy that we were playing for such a great club. I didn't need to be told that and I sent the book flying back across the table at him and then stormed out. But my reaction worked. He summoned us back into the meeting and agreed we could have the apartments we wanted. I don't know if he realised it, but I was on the point of walking out and heading back home. I would have done it, too, because by this time Beverley was really unhappy. Also, Milan had broken their promise to me and that wasn't good enough. Still, it was sorted out just a few weeks before the derby game and the one bone of contention I still had was about a car. The day after I scored against Inter I had a silver Mercedes delivered . . . obviously just a coincidence.

With off-field matters settled, things became better and better. I had a strong relationship with the fans and we reached the final of the Italian Cup even though we missed out on a UEFA Cup place when we ended fifth in the championship.

The final, over two legs, was another disappointment. We had beaten Inter in the semi-final and then had to play Sampdoria, who had Graeme Souness and Trevor Francis in their side at the time. Graeme scored the single goal in the first match at the San Siro and then we lost 2–1 in the second match at Genoa. After a bright start, the season ended on a low note – and some other off-field problems came up over advertising contracts which had been set up for me. Even when I thought things had been organised, there was always something to disturb my life at Milan. They were almost always solved satisfactorily – but they were a nuisance. The one good thing from them was that they toughened me up for what lay ahead.

Another bonus was that we *did* get into the UEFA Cup because the team which had kept us out originally, Sampdoria, now found themselves in the European Cup Winners Cup. So while I had to be content with a runners-up medal from my first club final, I did have the European stage to look forward to. We did okay, reaching the third round before going out to the Belgian side, Waregem.

By then, though, the club was in turmoil and the results on the field were secondary to the crises which kept hitting AC Milan off the field. That UEFA Cup defeat brought it all to a head – unbelievably, Milan were close to bankruptcy. I had had my own worries, too, with injuries and things looked bleak. Only a money-spinning run to the UEFA Cup final could have saved the president from going. At the last gasp, when the club seemed to be facing closure and it had been explained to us that we would all become free agents, Berlusconi arrived on the scene like the Seventh Cavalry riding to the rescue. His timing was perfect. Hours before bankruptcy would have been declared, he put forward his rescue package and Milan was saved. We celebrated on the field by defeating Fiorentina and playing some magnificent football. The new man in command, Berlusconi, was reputedly one of Italy's richest men. He had saved our footballing futures – or so it seemed at the time of his rescue package.

Sadly, it did not turn out that way for me. When he arrived my time in Italy was drawing to a close. He had his own ideas about the way the new Milan should go. He had saved the club with a huge injection of cash and it was, quite simply *his* club. He owned it and he wanted to run it in *his* way. He wanted bigger names and bigger stars, and at the end of that season he went into the transfer market and bought the three Dutchmen who were going to be the architects of the new Milan.

But Berlusconi had a couple of problems which didn't make things easy for him. The Dutch players – Marco van Basten, Ruud Gullitt and Frank Rijkaard – could not come to the club that season. He had to wait a whole year before they could join . . . and it was obvious to everyone that when they arrived I was on my way out. That was his second headache, because I was popular with the support. If I remained in the team and kept scoring goals, they wouldn't be all that happy at the thought of my leaving the club.

And so began my worst period in Italian football and my first taste of behind-the-scenes politics, the kind which can wreck careers. On this occasion the career at risk was mine, because no matter how well I played, I was leaving. And to make sure I would not be missed too much by the fans, I was axed for game after game. It didn't matter that I was the best striker at the club: Berlusconi wanted the support to be conditioned to seeing the team without me. So I would train all week and then I'd report for games and I'd know that Nils Liedholm had picked me and then in the dressing-room the team would suddenly be changed and I would be left out. It was a bad time and an embarrassing time. Poor Liedholm used to come up to me in the dressing-room and put his arm round my shoulders and then tell me I was not playing. He hated doing it, but with Berlusconi in charge, he had no alternative. He had to do it.

But, for all his power, Berlusconi could not wipe me out of the fans' memories. They still wanted me in and when I did play, they still cheered me. Even the last time I played they were behind me when I was sent off after a brawl against Udinese when I caught Colovatti a dull one. I just wellied and he went down and then there were four or five of them round me having a go and I popped the 'keeper and I knew I was going off. All the months and months of frustration had boiled up in me that day and so I left Italian football the way I had entered it – with a red card. Ordered off in my first match and my last. Some going.

That wasn't the end I wanted. Far from it. But the pressure on me throughout that season had been immense. I was just a pawn in the power game being played by Berlusconi. The Dutchmen were coming and I had to go. Even then, the president made sure that I left Italy when I was sold. There was no way he wanted me back at San Siro.

I was not the only victim. Ray left, too, and the season after that, Nils Liedholm had gone. Arrigo Sacchi, now the national team boss, was plucked from some obscure club and handed the reins. He was eventually handed all the credit for changing the face of Italian football – but I have never seen it that way. Sacchi is reputed to be the man who began the 'pressing game' in midfield and who liberated the game from the dead hand of *cattanaccio*. But Liedholm had preached the same tactics all the time I played under him. He also moved into a zonal marking system and the things he attempted with the team I played in were later adopted by Sacchi. I still like to think that I was in at the start of the changes which led to the attacking play you see now when you look at the Serie A games on television on a Sunday afternoon. Yes, there are things we should learn from them as I have said elsewhere in the book – but we should not sell our game short. Liedholm admired many of the British traits, like old-fashioned centre-forwards. And he tried to adapt those things he admired about our game and use them in Italy.

Liedholm didn't go all the way – he simply took some of the things he liked and grafted them on to the Italian way. For instance, he still used Franco Baresi as the sweeper and that's something you would never tamper with, especially as Baresi is probably the best defender in world football.

Anyhow, Sacchi carried on the work Liedholm had begun, and when he went to the national team Fabio Capello took over and Milan are still playing the same way. Fabio was at the club as one of the coaches when I was there and he was a bit of a disciple of Liedholm. He liked what he saw then and he has continued to use some of Liedholm's ideas. It did not surprise me when Fabio got the job. He was groomed for it by Berlusconi. He was a member of the coaching staff and Berlusconi took him away from the club for a spell to work in other parts of his very extensive business empire. Then, after a year out spent broadening his managerial experience, he returned to Milan and took over when Sacchi got the job as national team boss. He was always a nice bloke and I got on well with him when I was there at the club. He was learning English then and I always had the impression that he would go on to greater things – and there he is in charge of one of the biggest clubs in Europe. But I always wonder just how he handled the interference which must come from the president. It cannot be easy when Berlusconi goes out to buy the stars and then Fabio, or whoever is running the team, has to fit them into the side.

I felt for Jean-Pierre Papin when he first went to Milan because he went through a period much like the one I had to endure. Sitting in the stand or on the bench is no joke no matter how much money you are making. You heard that Papin was unhappy, and I could identify with that. The difference was, though, that Berlusconi bought Papin. He wanted him. He didn't want me and that's how I ended up being sold to Monaco where the living was easy and the game less pressured.

Looking back now, I realise that he unintentionally did me a favour. Monaco was a good career move for me and it was Berlusconi who sold me there and made sure I would leave Italy. But I still think it's a helluva way to run a football team, no matter how much success the club gets. Football should be run by the professional managers – not by tycoons who see a club as little more than a new toy.

CHAPTER EIGHT

A Fistful of Medals

You can ask any footballer in any country in the world what he wants from the game during his career and I think you will always get the same answers, because no matter where you are, attitudes among players don't alter that much.

You want success when you are a youngster. As you grow more mature, you also look for long-term security for your family and yourself. Then, when that has been achieved, you also want to have a fistful of medals to rekindle memories once you have stopped playing.

I was no different from any other player in this respect. At Coventry and then at Portsmouth I was searching for success, for a chance to win honours and, maybe, a chance to win medals too. When I moved on to Milan, some success had been achieved because I was in the England team – and then in my first season there we reached the final of the Italian Cup. But after that match I ended up with a losers' medal and that was not exactly what I had in mind . . .

Still, I did have the financial security for the future that I had been looking for by the time I moved on to Monaco. In my first season there I helped the team win the French Championship which meant that after about ten years as a professional I had just one medal to show for all the games and all the globe-trotting.

Again, I wanted more but then injury struck and my career was put on hold. And that's when Graeme Souness stepped back into my life and opened the door I had been looking for – it was a door clearly marked 'For Winners Only' – and this time I needed very little persuasion to push my way through it. There is no doubt that Graeme used the lure of winners' medals and the almost-constant Euro-presence of a club such as Rangers to lure me to Ibrox.

Not that I needed too much convincing by then. The exploits of Rangers under Graeme's guidance had penetrated most levels of European football by then. And I was probably more aware of this than others because I had watched them with interest after turning down the chance of going there first time round. Graeme had made an enormous impact on the club and his bold initiative in signing top English international players was something which underlined to me his ambitions. So many of these ambitions were being realised as the seasons swept past . . .

And I knew that I could have been a part of some of the Ibrox triumphs. Now the chance was there again and, as I say, Graeme painted a picture of Championship medals and Cup medals and big games in the European Cup, and I knew that this was another time for a career decision to be made – and, hopefully, another chance to make a decision which would be right for me.

Thankfully that's how it has turned out. All the moves I made did work out but few of them have worked out as well as the one to Rangers. Portsmouth gave me experience I needed but turned out to be no more than a one-season stepping-stone, though that's not how I first envisaged it. Milan took me into the greatest League in the world, boosted my international reputation and gave me long-term security, but ended in tears with the arrival of Silvio Berlusconi as the owner of the club. Monaco gave me a glamorous lifestyle and my first winners' medal, but ended sadly because of the injuries I had there.

Rangers have brought me all that I wanted after that. The medals have arrived – just as Graeme promised – and the football has been marvellous, the crowds have been tremendous and Beverley and the kids and myself all love living in Scotland. And I can look at a whole lotta lovely winners' medals from all three domestic trophies. We have been able to lift the jinx which hung over Graeme during his years in charge – when he could not add the Scottish Cup to the other trophies he won so consistently.

Anyway, I can still remember the first medal I collected – and it was just a few months into my new career with Rangers. It was the last Sunday in October 1990 to be precise, and the previous season had been a bad one by the high standards which Graeme and Walter Smith had set at Ibrox since taking over. They had won the title again, but had lost in the final of the Skol Cup to Aberdeen and had been knocked out in the second round proper of the Scottish Cup by Celtic. That was not what the fans had been used to and so there was a lot at stake when we went back into a Skol Cup final at Hampden against Old Firm rivals Celtic. But, I must say, that was the kind of challenge I relished. It was another reason why I had come to Rangers. I wanted *big* games, I wanted games where you could feel the tension sweep down from the terracings and stands, the kind of games I never did get in the so sedate surroundings of Monaco.

We had just gone out of Europe too, out in the second round of the European Cup against Red Star of Belgrade. That had been a body blow to the fans and to us players, even though we realised before the supporters did that we had lost to a class act. That was proved when Red Star went on to lift the trophy that year by beating Marseille in a penalty shoot-out.

That, though, was in the future. As we approached the Hampden game with Celtic it was very fresh in our minds that we had lost to them in the Scottish Cup just a few months earlier and that we had crashed out of Europe early. Celtic had had no such problems. They hadn't been in Europe and so had not had that diversion, and they must have felt that they had the Indian sign over us in the Cup.

When they took the lead through their centre-half, Paul Elliott, their fans began to celebrate as if the cup was already won. Against another team they would perhaps have been right. On another day against Rangers they might even have been right. But on that Sunday afternoon, too many of us were playing to lift the problems which had been surrounding the club. As well as the Red Star blow, the club captain, Terry Butcher, had had a highly publicised row with Graeme Souness after Terry had been dropped for the semi-final of the Skol Cup when we defeated Aberdeen. More controversy had followed that when Graeme and Terry had another bust-up in the week before the final. They were troubled times and there were still some sounds of booing from the fans upset at my arrival – but not too many that day, though, because Coisty was in the team with me.

But, after fifty-two minutes, we had to accept that we were behind and that Celtic looked like adding to our misery. That feeling did not last too long, however. Within thirteen minutes Mark Walters had grabbed the equaliser and the game was forced into extra time. And it was during that period of play that Richard Gough scored the deciding goal. It killed off Celtic, revitalised us and there I was, within months of joining the club, holding one of the medals that Graeme had promised me.

The weeks when I had suffered those jeers from the fans didn't matter any more. By now they were dying out and all I wanted was to go on winning and winning and winning . . .

With a few hiccups along the way, that's more or less what we did in my first season with the club. We did go out of the Scottish Cup to Celtic in that now rather infamous game where I was sent off along with Terry Hurlock and Mark Walters. It wasn't the happiest day for me that one; to be shown the red card in a quarter-final tie at Parkhead was not the type of thing I needed. The game was lost, we were out, and I felt for the first time the desolation which defeat in an Old Firm game leaves in its wake. Thankfully I have not had that feeling too often.

Injuries and suspensions began to bite deep into the team's resources after that, and then Graeme Souness left the club to go back to Liverpool as manager. The run-up to the title was underway. Aberdeen were challenging us so strongly that it looked like going all the way down to the wire. On this occasion that meant a shoot-out between ourselves and Aberdeen at Ibrox on the last day of the season. Normally that was something all of us would have settled for quite happily. This time, though, things were different. Our results began to slip a little, and as well as Walter having to take over from Graeme so late in the day, he had to contend with terrible injuries. Our captain, Richard Gough, didn't play in the last three matches for instance. He was suspended when we sneaked a win at Paisley against St Mirren in the closing minutes with a goal from young Sandy Robertson . . . and then he was downed by a bout of hepatitis and ruled out of the last two matches against Motherwell at Fir Park and against Aberdeen at home. Goughie had to listen to the games while lying in a hospital bed.

The first result could have done nothing to help his recovery. We were well beaten by Motherwell, on a high themselves because they were in the Scottish Cup final after beating Celtic on a penalty shoot-out at Hampden in the semi-final clash. In other seasons Fir Park might have been a place to pick up a couple of points or even a single point, but that day we crashed to a 4–2 defeat and suddenly, from leading the title race, we had fallen behind Aberdeen. They didn't have to come to Ibrox to win any more. All they had to do was come to Ibrox and get one point – something that they are always capable of doing at any ground in the country.

When we looked at the walking wounded around the stadium in the days leading up to the game, things did look bleak. But we had to dig deep into our own personal resources as players, as Rangers players, to overcome all the obstacles. It was a tough time for everyone: tough for the players; tough for the fans who were dreaming of another title win; and toughest of all for Walter Smith and his assistant, Archie Knox, who had now arrived at the club from Manchester United.

They had to get us in the right frame of mind. They had to pick the team from the remnants of the squad left to them, and they had to prove themselves a winning partnership at the same time. I think that taking over from any manager who has been successful is always a hard thing to do. Taking over from someone whose track record was as good as Graeme's had been was an immense task. Rangers were lucky to have Walter in place, with the added bonus that Walter could take Archie away from the biggest club in England.

The way Walter handled that crisis - and as we approached the game, it was obvious that it *was* a crisis – was the confirmation that he would grow into the great manager he has since become. I'm not trying to suggest in any way that it was a make-or-break situation for Walter and

Archie. It wasn't that. But it would have been a major blow to both of them if they had lost that title after being in the lead with only a handful of games left. They must have known that themselves, but throughout the week their time was spent taking the pressure away from us. They made sure that things were right for the lads who were going to play even though, day after day, there seemed to be some new injury problem. It must have been a nightmare for the pair of them. But now, looking back, I'm sure they must realise that the troubles they had then and the way they were able to overcome these difficulties gave them the best preparation they could have had for the seasons which lay ahead. None of us were in any doubt when Walter was appointed that he was the man for the job. That week he underlined our belief in him by the way he handled everything the fates threw at him.

Terry Hurlock ended up playing at left-back in the match, probably for the first time in his career. John Brown was not anywhere near fit but, Bomber being Bomber, responded when the call to the colours arrived and he was there to add his experience to the defence.

There was a huge crowd that day and the Aberdeen fans arrived in party mood – before half-time I was able to dampen them down a bit with a goal. And then I scored a second and we had done it. Before the game a lot of players had written us off. They had looked at the injuries to key players, examined the upheaval there had been at the club and compared our recent form with that of Aberdeen, making up their minds that there was to be no three title wins in a row for Rangers. We had other ideas.

It was a bit of a watershed win, that one, I think. After that it was always going to be 'Walter's team' as opposed to the team Graeme had built. Walter was going to bring in some of his own players and he was able to do that with the confidence and backing of the supporters who had seen him snatch back the title just as Aberdeen seemed to have a certain grip on the trophy.

It was a milestone for me, too. As well as getting my second medal I knew that from that match onwards I would be accepted by the supporters. Any tiny pockets of resistance which might have just hung on had now been won over. And it didn't matter who was going to partner me in future – I was my own man. I was Mark Hateley of Rangers. Not just another player who might have come up to the club for a year or two and then thought about moving on. I felt a part of the place, and though Graeme had gone, his promise of medals had been kept in my very first season.

In a way, the problems we had had to face up to hardened me even more. I had arrived with respect for the Scottish game – but my respect had grown over the season. And the nail-biting finish and that earlier Skol Cup final win over Celtic as well as the defeat by them in the Scottish Cup had shown me in no uncertain manner just how competitive things could be. The lads in England who thought it was a one-horse race should have been asked to take part in these three games alone. They would have changed their views very, very quickly.

It may have seemed a little easier since then but when you examine the games closely you reach the same conclusion over and over again. No one gives an inch in the Premier League. They are all, and I do mean all, out to knock us off our perch. In my second season Hibs did it when they beat us in the semi-final of the Skol Cup. It was at a time when the new players brought in by Walter were still settling in, still learning what it was all about to be a Rangers player, I expect. We lost in that match at Hampden, we went out of Europe rather unluckily to Sparta Prague (a team I believe we would have beaten had we met them later in the season), and it was only after these set-backs that it all started to come together. All the little elements which Walter and Archie worked on began to produce the team which did so wonderfully well in the 1992–93 season.

There was another little bit of a breakthrough in that season, too – we won the Scottish Cup. For the first time in eleven years, the old trophy could be decorated in red, white and blue ribbons and carried back to the Trophy Room at Ibrox. It was a great feeling for us all – but more so for the lads who had suffered during the long run without success in that particular tournament. Not one player who had been in that Cup-winning side – it was a 4–1 win in a replay against Dundee United – was left. The strange thing, though, was that the backroom was full of losing Dundee United men from that 1981 final. Davie Dodds and Billy Kirkwood had both played – and Walter had been the assistant manager at Tannadice then.

Between times Rangers had lost in two finals to Aberdeen and then in another to Celtic. Mostly, though, the team had gone out in the early rounds and the fans were sure that we were jinxed. It was the one domestic trophy Graeme Souness did not win in his time with the club and we were all acutely conscious of this. And when that year's tournament kicked off it looked as if the jinx theory might have some substance.

The draw for the first round proper was against Aberdeen at Pittodrie. I was forced to sit out the game because of injury, but the lads rose to the occasion and Coisty scored and that solitary goal was enough to push us beyond the Aberdeen challenge and into the next round.

There was very little respite for us in the next round, though. The one bonus we did get was that we had a home draw, and in the Cup you learn how important that can be – particularly against Premier League opposition. We found ourselves up against Motherwell, the holders. They had gone almost forty years without a Cup success until beating Dundee United in 1991. Now they wanted a taste of more glory and they took the lead in yet another match I had to watch from the stand. Phil O'Donnell scored their goal in the first half and it was Alexei Mikhailichenko who grabbed the two goals which sent us into the tournament quarter-final.

More Premier League opposition waited for us there in the shape of St Johnstone, and for this match we had to travel again. This time I was able to play and I helped in a 3–0 win which was a little easier than we had expected. Coisty inevitably scored the first, Goughie got the second and I helped myself to the third.

Suddenly it was the semi-final with ourselves, Celtic, Airdrie and Hearts in the draw. The cynics pointed out that the Old Firm rarely clash in a semi and that a final between the two of us was certain. They got it wrong this time. We met Celtic – another Cup game I missed – and we had David Robertson sent off early in the match for a foul on Joe Miller and that old hoodoo looked to have struck once more. The lads, though, worked so hard and played so well that when Coisty scored I knew we had won. It was a ten-man victory (which we would repeat eighteen months later at our own place) and it was a crucial win for us.

The Championship is always first choice when you are looking at the trophies you can aim for during any given season. By this time we had made sure of winning that, and the Scottish Cup, so elusive for so long, was waiting for us. Shock team of the season Airdrie, who had been tipped for relegation by some, were our opponents. They had beaten Hearts after a replay and a penalty-kick decider when their nerve held better than the Tynecastle team and reached a national final six months after claiming they were robbed of a place in the Skol Cup final by a highly controversial refereeing decision. They were organised, hard players and no mugs. They proved that to us in the final. We won and we did so after being two goals ahead by half-time. I had got the first after half an hour – in only my second Cup appearance of the season – and Coisty scored the second right on the interval. But we could not shake them off. Andy Smith scored for them ten minutes from the end and they forced us right to the final whistle. But it was another medal – and by scoring on each of my appearances I felt I deserved it – and it was a very important medal. It was the twenty-fifth time that the club had won the Scottish Cup and after that eleven-year wait it was all the better to savour victory.

So, there I was, four medals in two seasons and looking for more. Even then I was not able to grasp what was going to happen in that third medal-hunting season.

We wanted the title again, we wanted a long run in Europe for a change, we wanted the Scottish Cup again and the League Cup again – we wanted everything. And we came so close to getting everything. It was an epic season and one which must have put this team into football history as one of the best ever Ibrox sides. Only a few teams have won the treble and only one has taken a European trophy. We took the treble and went undefeated in the European Cup. It still seems incredible. But I can look at the medals and believe it quite easily as I look back at some of the games which formed that roll of honour . . .

The Skol Cup win over Aberdeen stands out in the early part of the season because it was a game which sneaked up on us almost unnoticed. That might sound like a strange thing to say about a major Cup final but it was true. We came right off our European Cup win over Leeds United at Elland Road and all the hysteria which had surrounded the two games against the English champions to head for Hampden and a clash with the team who were to snap at

119

our heels all season. It's a fairly well-known football fact that teams returning to domestic football after a demanding European game often slip a little. It is natural, at times, for that to happen. But for us the normal rules did not apply too often as we went searching for the success we wanted. And they didn't apply that Sunday in October either. Even though the game dragged into extra time we were still able to get the goal which gave us the first part of the treble we were chasing. Stuart McCall edged us in front only quarter of an hour or so into the game and then, in the second half, Duncan Shearer levelled things. It was well into extra time – maybe around six minutes before a penalty shoot-out would have been necessary – when Gary Smith knocked a try from me past his own 'keeper. It was enough, and we were on course for glory . . .

We had the title race to concentrate on and the games in the Champions' League to play before the Scottish Cup began. There was breathing space before then, but there was no room for error. In fact, we lost just four games in the League during the season and yet Aberdeen never left our heels. They nagged away at us constantly, and while people were tipping us for an early win in the title race at one stage, the men from Pittodrie held on so grimly that it was at Airdrie in May before the title was claimed. We lost two of our games after that fifth successive title win and after going out in Europe too I'm sure that Walter must have feared some kind of reaction in the Scottish Cup. There was none.

Again we found ourselves having to play Aberdeen in the final after a march through the other rounds which had been slightly easier than the season before. The main problem was that we didn't play a single game at our own ground. We were away against Motherwell for the first tie where Coisty scored twice in our 2–0 win, then down to Somerset Park for a clash with Ayr United and another comfortable 2–0 win with Coisty getting another and Dale Gordon also grabbing one. It was new territory for me in the next round, too, when we headed up to Arbroath just a few days after returning from Bruges – not much difference between the Belgian ground and little Gayfield but that's the romance of Cup football. We won again – 3–0 this time – and we were suddenly in the semi-final of the tournament without losing a single goal. We did lose one at Parkhead against Hearts, but big Dave McPherson and that man Coisty again were the scorers. My tally so far had been just one against Arbroath where Alastair and Neil Murray had helped themselves to the others. So now we were in the final and my front-line partner had scored in every round. Didn't he just love that?

Then, just when he might have managed to put himself into the record books yet again, tragedy struck. He broke his leg playing in that disastrous World Cup game against Portugal and was out for the rest of the season. I knew how he was feeling. I'd been down that road, that long, lonesome injury road. And I had had to sit out important games when you feel you could be there helping the lads. It's a lousy feeling and, while Coisty is great at putting a brave face on things, he was hurting inside. I knew that because I had been through the same thing at Monaco with my series of injuries there.

It was probably worse for Alastair because we were hitting the climax of the season. He would have missed the European Cup final, for example, if we had qualified – and we were close. And he did miss out on the deciding title game and the Cup final. It was a blow for us, too . . .

Our partnership in Europe had been fairly constantly interrupted either through injuries or, eventually, my suspension for the last two Champions' League games. Now the closing stages of the League and the Cup final saw us split again. The title was settled a full month before our date with Aberdeen at Parkhead – Hampden was now closed for rebuilding and so the match was to be played at the ground of our Old Firm rivals.

Following the Championship clincher at Broomfield we lost two of our next three matches while Walter switched the team around to keep us fresh for the final. One of them was against Aberdeen up at Pittodrie and we lost 1–0. They must have thought they had caught us on the way down after all the heady days of Europe and the satisfaction at taking title number five. It must have given them hope that, in a season where they had been the one team to mount a consistent challenge to us, they would not finish empty-handed. But all their hopes died in the first half that day. Tired we might have been; disappointed over Europe we most certainly were: but our hunger for success remained undiminished. We were, after all, now playing to complete the treble, something only a handful of Rangers teams before us had been able to do. Young Neil Murray, who had done so well when brought into the European ties, scored the first goal in the twenty-third minute, and two minutes before half-time I scored after Durranty sent me through on goal. They did have a little bit of a revival in the second half when Lee Richardson scored for them with a dozen or so minutes left. After that we defended and we defended as well as we had done all through that epic season, and the Cup was collected to be taken back to Ibrox for more celebrations.

Coisty was out on the field, hirpling around with us on the lap of honour and receiving the cheers of our support in the 50,000 crowd. He might have missed that match but his earlier goals in the Cup run deserved a special accolade. It was the first time since 1978 that the club had completed the hat-trick of domestic trophies, and the performances all through the season had given the fans a year they will never forget.

In fact, it was a year that none of us at the club will ever be able to forget. And, on a personal note, my medal tally had risen to seven in three incredible years. All that Graeme Souness had promised me had come true.

CHAPTER NINE

Happier Times with England

The best of times, the very best of times I had with England, were probably right back at the beginning of my career. Back when I was just a raw boy still playing in the English Second Division but clinching that move to Milan via a goal in the Maracana Stadium in Rio. The stuff dreams are made of, indeed, and looking back over the disappointments since, it seems all so long ago and far away . . .

I'd had my little bits of success with the Under-21 team, and Bobby Robson, then boss of England, promoted me to the full side. First of all he drafted me into the squad to face Scotland at Hampden back in May 1984. I went up to Glasgow but I didn't play, and I thought that would be my chance of making the full side finished until the following season. Sure, England were going on a South American tour, but I did not expect to be included in the élite group of players. I was still, so I thought, an apprentice. Bobby had other ideas – and other plans for me when he was hit by injuries. I'd had ten minutes against Russia at Wembley but nothing more, and now I was being catapulted into a tour which was to include games against Brazil, Uruguay and Chile.

It was all hard for me to grasp then, but I was helped enormously by the rest of the squad. The feeling in the group was good and I was rooming with Gary Stevens who is now at Ibrox with me. I'd played with him in the Under-21 team and we were mates, and so this was something else which helped me settle into the squad.

So much happened that there is still a strange feeling about it all, almost an unreal feeling, when I try to recall exact details of the game. I do remember that Brazil made a great play of being without some of their top players – Socrates, Falcao and Zico all missed the match. But we had players who had been left at home, too. That was the main reason I was there, wasn't it?

Bobby decided to play with two wide men, Mark Chamberlain and John Barnes, with myself and Tony Woodcock as the strike-force. It worked like a dream and we won 2–0, beating the Brazilians at their own attacking game on their own patch. John Barnes and I shared the goals – we share a birthday too, you know – and suddenly our reputations soared. There could not be a better place to make an impact than Maracana with its huge crowds and its knowledgeable fans. They weren't too happy with their own team that day, but I think they did recognise that England had come to attack and had done so. That's why we won the game . . .

In the next match Bobby tinkered about with the team a little bit – it was a tour designed to allow him a few experiments – but the team did not gel in the same marvellous fashion as it had against the Brazilians. In Montevideo against Uruguay we were brought back to earth with a 2–0 defeat. Then, in the last tour game in Santiago, we drew 0–0 with Chile.

The three games had been a success in spite of the one defeat. The games had all been played inside a week and we were far away from home, and yet we had been convincing in our approach to the matches. But while the goal I had scored stirred things up in Milan, it didn't provide me with any guarantee of a permanent England place – as I found out early the next season. By now I was a Milan player but had still to make my league début for the Italians. Whether that influenced the England manager, I don't know. All I do know is that in the Wembley clash with East Germany I was back on the bench and Paul Mariner was in the main striker's role. In the last ten minutes I took over from Tony Woodcock and Bryan Robson scored the one goal of the game. I returned to Italy wondering if a regular spot was going to be handed to me or not.

The next game was a month away and it was the opening World Cup game in the qualifying group for the Mexico finals of 1986. Now I was playing regularly in the Italian First Division and I had been scoring goals, and I suppose that influenced Bobby Robson to throw me in against Finland. Getting goals in Italy was not the easiest thing to do and it was impressing the people back home. Bobby had to be one of them. This was my first time playing in the World Cup and, just like my Maracana début, it was a dream beginning for me. In fact, it could not have been better if I had written the script myself.

It was like a holiday for me after having to face the packed defences in Italy. No sweeper system and none of the ruthless tackling I had had to contend with in my opening matches in Serie A. I kept up my scoring streak, too. I was able to notch up two of the five goals in our win, with the others going to Tony Woodcock, Kenny Sansom and Bryan Robson.

As always, there were those who tried to downgrade the win, saying it was 'only' Finland we were playing – but the Finns, like other smaller countries, could pose their own problems at times. That night at Wembley we just didn't give them the chance to frustrate us. It was my first full game at Wembley and it was tremendous to get off to a flier in front of the English fans. That's the kind of thing I spent my boyhood dreaming about. Now it had come true and it had all happened so quickly. Just a few months earlier I had been playing in the Second Division with Portsmouth and thousands of the fans who were at Wembley that night had scarcely heard of me. I remember thinking how incredible the change in my life had been.

Within a month things had changed again and my England career was interrupted once more. I damaged my knee against Torino, needed an operation, and actually *had* the operation the very day England played Turkey in Istanbul in another World Cup tie. Peter Withe took my place and we won 8–0 – an amazing result at international level. There was a good rapport among the lads in that squad back then and that helped get the results. But I do recall wondering if the injury would hold back my England career.

The worries were needless. Bobby Robson picked me to play against Northern Ireland the following year in Belfast and we won 1–0 and I got the goal. I was in and out of the team fairly regularly from then on, sometimes scoring, sometimes not. But I always felt that Bobby had me marked down as a member of his squad and that was comforting.

One of the games I enjoyed playing was against Italy in a tournament in Mexico City the summer before the finals were held there. My rival from Inter, Colovatti, was playing and I knew it would be a right battle between us. None of my team-mates from AC Milan were in the team, though, and the Italian side eventually won 2–1 thanks to a lousy penalty decision given against Gary Stevens. It was a liberty. We had been a goal down and then I had equalised and the game looked sure to end in a draw until the Mexican ref decided on the penalty, which Altobelli scored. We were disappointed by the result but I was not disappointed in the way we had played. I knew the Italians and I knew that they were determined to hold on to the World Cup they had won in Spain three years earlier. To do so well against them was a boost to our own hopes.

On a personal level, I had continued my scoring run with the side with two goals in three games. The first was that so important goal which gave us a draw in Helsinki against the Finns – yes, the same Finnish team the cynics had dismissed when we destroyed them at Wembley but who had now become more determined and more organised when they played at home. We were a goal behind after five minutes and had to contend with one of the worst surfaces I'd ever been asked to play on in senior football. My equaliser was vital and it meant a lot to me after my injury and fitness problems with Milan towards the end of their season. It was a good job we did get that result because the tour games brought nothing but disappointment at the start.

We had lost to Scotland before leaving – Goughie scored. Then we lost to Italy and Mexico, and the tour was only rescued by a 3–0 win over West Germany. We needed that result badly but, by that time, I had had to fly home to be ready to play for Milan, and Kerry Dixon scored two goals, increasing the pressure on me to keep my place. It's a funny thing about playing international football: one bad game can see a player axed. One bad result can see a team crucified. That doesn't happen in the same way at club level.

But I knew that I had to take up any challenge, no matter who it came from, because I was determined to be a part of the squad which went back to Mexico for the World Cup finals. What I didn't know at that time was that the greatest adventure of them all would turn sour for me, too.

En route to the finals we had altitude training at Colorado Springs and then played some games against Mexico in Los Angeles and Canada – who were also in the finals – in Burnaby. We won them both and I scored the goals to stake my claim for the finals themselves. We defeated Mexico 2–0 and I was the scorer of both goals. Then we beat Canada 1–0 and it was my goal which brought victory again. I felt good. I felt in the right frame of mind for the matches in Mexico where we were in the same group as Portugal, Morocco and Poland. We knew the problems we would face from the altitude and the worries over the food and the drinking water and all the rest of it. Basically, it was not the place most footballers would have chosen as the venue for the greatest show on earth. But we had to get on with it. And, as I said, I felt good and the two results we had had confirmed the form and the spirit of the team.

Then the matches started and things began to go wrong. These tournaments are never easy, mainly because of the burden of expectations of the people back home and the failure to realise how difficult the opposition can be. There are very few easy touches in World Cup football. You can get the odd ones like San Marino or Estonia or Latvia during the qualifying matches, but once in the finals every team is a quality opponent and World Cups have been littered with shock results down through the years.

We lost our opener to Portugal 1–0, and we could only draw with Morocco 0–0. The pressure was on. It was piled on so heavily that I was one of the victims. I was dropped for the remaining group game against Poland and, in fact, after the Morocco game I was not to play a full game in the finals again. To some extent I felt that I had carried the can for those two poor results and I found that hard to take. I thought I had played okay; I had made chances for other people, which has always been a part of the game, but I hadn't been able to score myself and so I was left out even though I had not had too many scoring chances myself in the two matches. Things just had not gone right for us.

Then, against Poland, it clicked. Gary got a hat-trick and we were through to the knock-out stage. I was pleased for the lads and pleased for England, but I was annoyed and I told Bobby Robson. I just told him how let down I felt. I'd gone there as the main striker, scored the goals in the two warm-up matches and then, when things started to go a little bit wrong, I was out. I still think I could have played a part in the rest of the competition and I told him that, too. Not that it made the slightest bit of difference: Bobby listened but he wasn't going to do anything, was he? The team was on a bit of a roll and suddenly, from being pilloried by the press, they were all heroes. That can happen so often in this type of tournament. One result can make all the difference. It didn't matter that we had not topped the qualifying group and Morocco had. It was that we went on from the Polish match to take three more goals off Paraguay who had successfully stopped Belgium reaching the later stages. We won 3–0 again in that match, with Gary getting two goals and Peter Beardsley the other. I managed a brief appearance but I knew I'd slipped down the pecking order. It was a depressing time personally and Chrissie Waddle, who was sharing with me, worked hard to keep my spirits up. He was good but I was as down as I had ever been. It's a strange situation you can find yourself in: you are genuinely happy the team is doing well and that the lads are getting results – but you still want so much to be in there as a part of the whole thing.

Then it finished with that controversial goal from Maradona. The Hand of God? – I ask you. I wasn't even on the bench for that game when we met Argentina in the quarter-finals. I was sitting in the stands and the sun was shining straight into our faces, and at first I didn't know what had happened. Then I saw it on the television replays and it was so glaring, so obvious to everyone – and yet it was the goal which sent us home from the finals. It was cheating. It was just as bad as bribing someone. Then Maradona came out with all that nonsense and you knew then that he was a cheat. He was a wonderful player. When he first went to Napoli he was just incredible – but he had bad habits and they didn't change, and that is why he is back in Argentina now, trying to kickstart a career that he himself destroyed.

Looking back now, and taking away the fact that Maradona punched the ball into the net, I still have to blame Peter Shilton. There was this little fellow going up for a ball in the box with his arm raised and Shilts allowed him the time and space to get the ball past him and into the net. Shilts should have flattened him. He shouldn't have given Maradona the chance to cheat England that day. It was a sad end to what had started off so well for me . . . and it was the one and only time I made the World Cup finals.

I won caps after that. But mostly I was second choice now and the excitement of Rio had vanished. When the time came for the next European Championships in West Germany I made appearances as a substitute and this time, in spite of the poor results we had (we lost all three games), Bobby didn't change his front men. The next season I was injured at Monaco and my career looked to be more or less over. It had only really lasted for four years and, while Bobby kept in touch with me during my injury spell at Monaco, I knew I was never going to be ready for another bash at the World Cup. It would have been terrific to go back to Italy for the finals but, instead, I was recovering in Monaco and signing for Rangers. I played thirty-one times in that four-year run and if I had been free of injury the tally would have been higher. I had one more cap after that, when

Graham Taylor bowed to public opinion and put me in against Czechoslovakia. It could have been a fresh start but I knew that was not going to happen. Maracana happens once in a lifetime. It happened for me right at the start of my England career, just as the scoring début at Wembley came early on, too.

These are memories that I'll never forget, but with them come some regrets. I know I could have helped England beat Argentina in Mexico and I know I could have helped the team get to the finals in the United States, too. Obviously it wasn't meant to be and I've got Rangers and their various successes to help ease any of the disappointments I might still feel. I remember that or I think about the goal against Brazil, the goal that changed the whole course of my life, and I realise I have something that no one can ever take from me.

And something that few footballers can look back on.

CHAPTER TEN

A Step Back for the Future

The gap in my career when I was out for those eighteen months or more at Monaco have become a bit of a bonus the older I get. I had always insisted that I would train so hard that the two missing years could be tagged on at the end of my time in football. That's what I intend to get from the game. I believe that I can play for another three years at top level – and I mean European Cup level – and I want to be doing that with Rangers, of course. There is not another team I would ever think about playing for now. Once you have been at Ibrox, once you have tasted the success that the club reeks of and the ambition which is always there, you can't imagine yourself stepping down from that stage. And to leave to go to most other clubs would be a step down.

I will talk to Walter towards the end of my current contract and then see what happens. But I want to finish my career with Rangers and – here's a surprise for you all – I can see myself moving back into a defensive role as my career comes to a close. I've done it in emergency situations and I've done it in practice games at training and the like. To be honest, I've enjoyed it and I've felt comfortable enough doing it. I've already talked it all over with Walter and he thinks the same as I do that a step back can add extra time to your football life.

I know that some of you will be wondering how on earth a centre-forward can make that transition – but there have been other examples. John Charles was one, wasn't he, and I was often compared to him when I was in Italy. Basically, by playing as a striker, you learn the tricks of that particular trade and by playing against the best defenders in the world (as I did during my time in Italy) you learn about their game, too. When I moved to Italy I came up against guys like Brio and Colovatti, Gentile and Passarella, and in France I had quite a series of tussles with Basile Boli among others. In Scotland I've battled with Alex McLeish and with Dave McPherson when he was with Hearts, and with Paul Elliott when he was with Celtic. I gave them respect and I think they gave me respect. It's been a bit of a mutual admiration society at times. The fans in Italy used to love it when Colovatti and I went out on to the field and proceeded to kick lumps out of each other – and then have a drink together after it was all over. They couldn't quite fathom it out. But off the field we were buddies.

Anyhow, to get back to the point, I had to match wits with these players all through my career and so I know what defenders like and what they don't like. I know what is in a striker's mind when he has to face one of those guys, too. So there is always a good chance that I could second-guess anyone who was coming up against me if I made the move to centre-half.

It was always more difficult playing in Italy because the defenders there were the very best in the world, bar none. They had to be because the clubs went out and bought the top players for every position. My Milan experiences have helped me to be a better player here. I have now played against the man-for-man marking style and the zonal style and I can put the two of them together in my mind and cause problems for the opposing players. I try to take up deliberately false positions. It's hard for a defender to know what a good or bad position for a striker is. I try to move into goal-threatening areas but not into the ideal position to score. Defenders then follow me into these false positions and when they do, I then move into the position I really want to be in.

Basically, I attempt to lure defenders into space that I don't really want. That immediately gives you an advantage. You have them on edge, guessing and wondering what is happening. In a good team a ball is going to stay in wide positions for fairly long stretches of time. When that happens, your ploy has to be to get yourself into a position where two men are forced to mark you. If you can get in between the back players, you make room for others to come through from midfield. The job of striker in modern football is not just scoring goals. It also involves making goals for other players and opening up defences to allow midfielders or defenders to come through. You often act as a decoy . . .

I'd like to think that, as a defender, I would not be dragged into these false positions because from experience I would *know* by instinct where my opponent really wants to place himself. Good defending is about reading the game, just as good front play has to be. If you can do it in one position, you can do it in another – and you would have the benefit of the added knowledge you had picked up yourself if you swapped roles. It's a prospect which interests me, excites me even, at times. And there is always the powerful possibility that it could add a year or two to my shelf life.

As well as that I have tried to look after myself – something I learned to do in Italy. As you get older you always tend to look after yourself that little bit better – probably something to do with time running out on you. I was lucky, though, to pick up things while I was over in Italy. It's no coincidence that players there last longer in the game. It's no coincidence, either, that the British players who went out there have lasted longer, too. Graeme Souness played until his mid-thirties, Trevor Francis was the same, and Ray Wilkins is still playing for Queen's Park Rangers. Playing in Italy you learn a lot of little disciplines. Here at home, players can go for a couple of beers at the wrong time of the week. That just doesn't happen in Italy. They enjoy a beer or two just as we do – but only when they think it is right to take a drink. They just don't step out of line over there. I learned a lot from their self-discipline. You pick up things, add them to your own armoury and, if it works for you, you take it on board. If not, you discard that idea and try something else.

You learn all the time. I'm still learning – like watching defenders on the field. I like to rest a lot at home and on one night a week – usually Thursday – I like to go out and have myself four or five pints. That's the maximum and I've done it all through my career. Walter knows that is what I have done and he is happy enough to let me carry on with that little routine. I feel comfortable with it and it does nothing to harm my fitness. If I thought that it did, I'd change the habit of a lifetime. And I'd change quickly.

Of course, you also train better in Italy because you don't have the midweek grind of League football that we have to put up with in Scotland and England. You go into the team hotel on a Friday night which is at Milanello, the training ground. You stay there until the game on Sunday afternoon. You train on Friday, of course, and again on Saturday morning and then play snooker on the Saturday afternoon. Then on the Sunday afternoon you play. You don't have too many midweek games at all, so during the week you spend time on recovery training, or getting yourself clear of any knocks you might have picked up. We don't have time for that in Scotland – and yet I wouldn't swap things back again. I'm often asked if I miss Monaco and if I would like to be back living there, but we are all happy here in Scotland. Bev and the kids and I all think that this is home. We sold our house in England and cut our ties in that sense because this is where we want to live, where we want to put down roots after years of travelling around Europe.

Apart from the life off the field I do thrive on the cut and thrust of the games here and the way the competition gets tougher and tougher as we go on racking up success upon success.

There are problems with the game in Scotland. Too many matches is the obvious drawback. But I have enjoyed my time at Ibrox and I don't intend to leave in the near future.

The game is fast and it is physical – and I like that, too. You don't get very much time to put your foot on the ball in a Premier League match. Try it and you'll probably end up on your backside. But it is the kind of football the fans like. There are goals and incidents and there are tackles and physical contact which they enjoy, too. It's red-blooded football, hair-on-the-chest soccer, and if only we had fewer games then it would be near perfect for me.

Of course, you have to be ultra fit. That's where our pre-season training comes in. It started when Graeme was in charge but Walter has continued with the preparations in Italy and Il Ciocco. It's a typical training set-up as used by the Italian teams and it works well for us. I reckon our fitness levels are higher than those of any other team in Scotland after we have been to Il Ciocco. It's essential that they are because of the demands made on players. The management team have got it exactly right for us.

The Premier League Championship is the hardest trophy to win. For us it's like playing forty-four Cup finals in one season. It never gets any easier, either. It's only natural that teams want to topple us and so the matches are always tough. But you never get tired of winning and that's motivation enough for most of the lads. I can tell you from experience that you do get tired of losing and you get tired very, very quickly. Luckily that has never been a great issue at Ibrox since I've been a part of the side. Walter and Archie keep telling us that their job is to keep us happy and keep us motivated. But most top international players don't need too much motivation and so Walter and Archie try to keep the dressing-room atmosphere right. If things have gone wrong they are around to give us a gee or even a boot up the backside if that's what is needed.

We don't spend a lot of time on coaching and tactics because playing teams four or more times a season you tend to know what you are going to be up against every week. There is, I suppose, no great secret about the success we have had at Ibrox. Walter has put together a bunch of quality players and he lets us play. Nine times out of ten that is enough. Top players, international players – and that's what we have at Ibrox – don't have to be told too often how to play. Good players can grow on their own and develop on their own.

Walter and Archie and the rest of the backroom staff concentrate on keeping the training routines right, and on keeping the working atmosphere right. And it helps to know that they are just as hungry for success as all the players are. They want Rangers to succeed and so do we. We all want it just as much as the fans.

I think I stressed earlier how much of a collective thing it all becomes at Ibrox. It is not like any other club I have ever been with. Quite simply that is why there is no other club I want to go to. I'm only sorry that I didn't accept Graeme's earlier offers as I would have spent a few more seasons here enjoying more success than I had ever dreamed was possible.

CHAPTER ELEVEN

Hangover Time

When you come off a high there is always the chance that you can be hit by a slump in form. It's something that all successful teams have to guard against, and something that we, at Rangers, have been able to hold at bay in the past.

This season, 1993–94, was different. We had the kind of run that few clubs have ever been able to put together the year before – and that took its toll. We kicked off the new team with something like a dozen players still suffering from injuries and there is no doubt that some of these were the result of the demands placed on us all as we won the treble and marched unbeaten through the European Cup. Most of us played between fifty and sixty games that season; others who were also playing international football saw that total soar still higher, and so the stress and wear and tear of so much football exacted its price.

It also left me feeling gutted after our first-round European Cup defeat by Levski Sofia, who were not as good as any of the sides we played and defeated in last year's tournament. We went into the two games under strength – but, even then, we were in a winning position at Ibrox and remained poised to go through until an injury-time goal from them knocked us out in Bulgaria. It was hard to take and afterwards, for the first time in my career, I sat in the dressing-room thinking that time was running out on me. I have never felt that way before, and I do intend to keep playing at the highest level for another season or two. But because of the circumstances of the defeat I think I took it more badly than any loss I have experienced before. I suddenly thought to myself, 'You're not going to get too many more chances of winning the European Cup.' It was a strange sensation and I talked about it with Coisty and he said that he felt the same way. Both of us are on the wrong side of thirty; we're not ready for the knacker's yard, but we are getting on a bit. And to be knocked out so early by a bad side was a bitter, bitter blow.

The kind of desolation we felt was probably heightened by the memories of the Champions' League campaign and the expectations we all shared with the fans that we would be taking part in that mini-league of Super clubs once again. Yes, we could do it next year but it seems like a long, long time from now until the next tournament begins.

Between now and then we have a title to win and that never gets any easier. It remains our major target, however, and while we lost some ground at the start of the campaign we did not fall far behind. Given the team problems we had at the start of the season it has been encouraging for us that no one has been able to streak away at the top. If that had happened – if one of our main rivals had gone off on a run – then the outlook could be much worse than it is as I write this.

It has been a difficult time, not so much for the players as for the management staff. Walter Smith and Archie Knox are the men who have had to grapple with team selection as player after player went out through injury. They have had to try to adjust to the changes which have been forced on them in game after game. And they have also had to preach constantly to the squad about keeping up the high standards we had set before. It is easy for a player to become a little complacent when there is no threat to his first-team position, when no one is breathing down his neck. You know that only the very best performances can keep you in the side.

Last year everyone was wanting to play, so everyone was up for every match. No one wanted to miss out as big game followed big game with astonishing regularity. This season we have had a patchwork squad and disappointment followed disappointment, and Walter and Archie have had to hold the team together. It has been a much harder job for them this time round than it was when they were facing the cream of Europe, believe me.

Personally, I have simply tried to ignore the team problems, the injuries and the forced changes, because there is nothing that I can do about them. All I can do is play as well as I know how and as hard as I know how and hopefully help the side that way. I have worked hard to try to keep up the standard of performance which I have set for myself down through the years. Perhaps subconsciously I have been doing that a bit more in a bid to help some of the younger lads who played with me while Coisty was out. I scored a few more goals, too, which was nice. But it has been a rearguard action though at the end of it I expect the team to become even stronger than it was before. There are times when adversity can bring the lads together just as much as success does. Confidence can grow again as you battle together and when all the first-team squad lads are back together you sense that the hangover we have suffered will lift.

I doubt if any other countries put their players through such exhausting programmes as they do here in Britain. There are just too many games. It would have taken me almost two seasons in Italy or France to get to the number of matches I played last year. That surely can't be right. It's going to change next year and we will have eight games fewer in the Premier League programme, which will help. But a radical overhaul is required in Scotland and England if we are to match the rest of the world in skill. At the moment the time spent in Italy and France on skill training and ball work is much more frequent than here, and that is almost all down to the fact that there are so many midweek games that all you seem to do is play, train and try to recover from injury in time for the next match.

There has to be a better way. Until there is, we will always be handicapped at club level in Europe and at international level because of the physical demands made on players. This is not a case of making excuses for our poor start to the season. If we were out in front in the title race and still in Europe I would say the same.

Anyway, the time to make judgments on us as a team will be when everyone is back in place and when everyone is back to 100 per cent match fitness. As some of the lads have filtered back over the weeks confidence has been growing in the team as has the realisation that by the time Christmas comes around – the time when titles can often be won or lost – we'll be ready, given a decent share of the breaks. We must be due some luck by now. Whether we get that or not, we will prove to everyone that the European result and the early season losses were mistakes which have not damaged the spirit of the side. And have certainly not blunted the hunger of the team. There are more prizes to be won, more records to be established, and another chance to play in the European Cup for Coisty and me, I hope.

Levski remains the hardest result to accept, mainly, I suppose, because we have to wait so long to play in the tournament again. And also because we all knew it was a game we should have won and one we would have won if everyone had been fit. Normally, scoring three goals at home is a passport to the next round – you don't expect to be under any pressure when you go 2–0 up and then, after they score, get another right away. But in Europe games hang on a knife edge. The difference between success and failure can be a moment's loss of concentration. We allowed Levski a second goal at Ibrox and then over there, after Durranty scored, they hit us with a late, late goal.

I'd scored twice at home and then at the end these goals didn't matter. I know how the fans must have felt – but, if anything, I felt worse then they did. It's the lowest moment in my time with the club.

Hopefully, the set-backs will act as a spur to us for the remainder of the season. I know how I feel and I'm pretty certain that the rest of the lads feel the same. Rangers as a club have never been prepared to take second place to anyone. This team which now represents the club is exactly the same. We might have had a lot of success – but there is never going to be enough to satisfy any of us. Down through the history of the club there have been a lot of hard acts for us to follow, but we would like to be remembered as one of the truly *great* Rangers teams. We have gone part of the way towards that now and we won't stop until we can get that recognition.

That is very important to all of us.